DIGITAL TRANS FORMATION: THE INFINITE LOOP

BUILDING EXPERIENCE BRANDS FOR THE JOURNEY ECONOMY

PAUL MISER

DIGITAL TRANSFORMATION: THE INFINITE LOOP

BUILDING
EXPERIENCE BRANDS
FOR THE
JOURNEY ECONOMY

PAUL MISER

ILLUSTRATIONS AND COVER DESIGN BY
Dan Madinabeitia

PMP

Paramount Market Publishing, Inc.

www.JourneyEconomy.com

Paramount Market Publishing, Inc.
274 North Goodman Street, STE D-214
Rochester, NY 14607
www.paramountbooks.com
607-275-8100

Publisher: James Madden
Editorial Director: Doris Walsh

Copyright © 2021 Paul Miser
First published USA 2021
Printed in USA

Cataloging in Publication Data available
ISBN-10: 1-941688-72-1
ISBN-13: 978-1-941688-72-4
eISBN: 978-1-941688-73-1

To Nikki & Kaia

CONTENTS

ACKNOWLEDGMENTS

WHEN I set out to write this book, I wanted to simply communicate the vision that I've seen unfolding over the last two decades of my career. When putting my thoughts together, I spent a tremendous of time to reflect on the moments, experiences and people that have helped me throughout my career and through the book-writing process. I've been lucky enough to be at the forefront of the technology revolution over the last twenty years; and to have built a career around how these technologies transform business is no easy task. It has required a lot of risk, persistence and guidance on the part of the organizations and the people around me throughout my journey.

I would not be where I am today without my managers and mentors that I've had in my career. Thanks to Joe Grigsby for allowing me to transfer my passion for the new world of social media behaviors into a new career trajectory. To the original Hudson Rouge leadership team of Cameron McNaughton, Ina Watkins, Jon Pearce and Emily Shahady, thank you for giving me the chance to start and build the digital team. And to Scott Kavanagh for giving the momentum the space it needed to thrive around the world. And of course, to the amazing client guidance of Jim Peters with all the forms our projects took over the years.

Thanks to all who supported the launch and development of Chinatown Bureau—Marie Berry for taking the leap with me and Dave Knox, Michael Farmer and Jason White as the guiding voices along the journey. And to Himanshu Sareen for bringing Chinatown Bureau into the Icreon family.

Thanks to Dan Madinabeitia for talking through concepts of this book and for taking the time to read it many times along the way. Also, thanks for the book illustrations and cover design.

For the continued conversation about life, business and whatever I might be reading at the time, thank you Paul Heron for the guidance and laughs over the last seven years.

To my family and friends for listening to me over the years, guiding me to be true to myself and for giving me the foundation of the person that I have become. Without you, this journey would have never happened and without you, the journey could have ended long ago. For that, I am forever grateful.

Finally, thanks to you, the reader—the professional that continues to learn, grow and evolve. You have been the true inspiration throughout my career. And I can't wait to see what you do next.

INTRODUCTION & OVERVIEW

LITTLE did I know, what I was getting myself into would bring me to the future of business. Sure, the steps along the way were fun, shiny objects but were never really part of the actual business discussions. Until now. As the real paradigm shift is happening right before our eyes, we can plainly see that it's not a moment in time but the collection of all things that came before. And those businesses that had the foresight to allow people like me at the table early are the ones writing our collective future. The truth is, businesses that have embraced digital and technology as a competitive differentiator are creating exponentially more value than their counterparts. This progressive digital transformation has completely shifted the way businesses capture, create, and retain customers throughout the entirety of the relationship. From simple awareness creation to streamlining shopping to building personalized products and services to offering new business models, digital-enabled businesses are changing the way they view their role in their customers' lives. They are transforming their mindset from acquisition to membership and from marketing to relationship. This paradigm shift not only changes how customers view the brands they do business with, but it's also changing the way businesses view themselves. Businesses at the forefront of digital transformation are finding their opportunity to truly define their potential, outside of the historical market forces that tether traditional businesses to slow growth. Rather, these businesses are aspiring to become something more for their customers and the world.

But I'm getting ahead of myself. Let's rewind. How did we get here?

Throughout my almost twenty-year career, I've had the opportunity to build businesses and brands at the forefront of crucial technological shifts. However, against my better judgement, I've fought hard not to be pigeonholed as a "digital guy" or a "tech guy." But every time I tried to get away, I was pulled back into the digital fray out of necessity, and out of it being the right thing to do. From my early days in business school to my life as a consultant, working with small businesses, fast growing startups and Fortune 10 global brands, I've continually found myself at the inflection point where brand strategy and technology intersect. This has brought me, and you, to this moment, this paradigm shift, where technology is connecting brands closer to their customers' lives than ever before to build new value for the customer and the business.

Each step along this journey has provided me the valuable lessons businesses should learn to make digital transformation the future of their business, brand, and relationship with their customers. And these lessons allow us to see the teachings currently standing at our doorstep, ready for us to discover.

Lesson #1: It was 2003. We were still in the wake of the dot-com bubble and the future of the internet was in question. Was Clifford Stoll, right? Was is it all a fad? I was halfway through business school, getting an MBA with a

Management Information Systems (MIS) emphasis. The coursework for the emphasis was highly technical around mobile network development, corporate IT Infrastructure and programming, things that wouldn't begin to be strategic differentiators for another decade. So, while watching the business world unfold and the uncertainty of tech enabled businesses crumbling, I opted to not take the final course for the emphasis simply because I didn't want to be pigeonholed as a tech guy. However, this specialized knowledge started my career off with a technological and network-minded lens through which to view business and brand strategy. While making this decision (which, looking back was probably the wrong one), I performed my due diligence into why the dotcom bubble burst, outside of the runaway valuations which ultimately took it down, to see what could be learned in that moment in time. The promises made from many of the dotcom companies were missed because of simple product-market fit. The promises of value propositions that were made a decade too soon to become reality. The adoption and perception of the internet as a means of commerce, interaction and brand-building just weren't where they needed to be to fulfill the promises. Only through understanding the complexities of technology and infrastructure created in my MIS coursework, was I able to see through the situation as it was to understand a basic lesson of digital transformation. There needs to be product-market fit or at least an adoption level of a solution to make real business sense.

Lesson Learned: Promises Made, Promises Missed. When embracing digital transformation, the first step is to find product-market fit and the adoption needed for creating value.

Lesson #2: It was 2006. After a couple years in the corporate world, I started a marketing strategy agency that was positioned as an outsourced marketing department for small- to medium-sized businesses. The insight for the business was that these companies were started by passionate, knowledgeable operators and didn't have the leverage or media buying power as a means to grow their customer base. So, they had to do things differently. The premise of the business was to deliver strategies that established an organic growth model that leveraged the business owner's expertise as thought leadership along with technology to attract, create, and retain customers. At this time, the digital landscape was just entering the Web 2.0 world where social networks, blogs, and content sharing was beginning to take off in the mainstream. We helped our small- to medium-sized clients position themselves as experts in their marketplace through content strategy, development and sharing along with social media engagement. It may sound common in today's landscape, but at the time it was revolutionary and something that gave these small businesses a competitive edge to move quickly and embrace these new technologies for organic growth. It wouldn't be until years later that their larger competitors would try to use this approach for their brands.

Lesson Learned: Media isn't the only way to win. Digital creates the opportunity to connect in different ways. From social networks to targeted conversations, brands and businesses can become more than just an advertiser but a respected resource of information.

Lesson #3: 2010 was a transformative year for technology, brand building and my career. It was the moment where I started to embrace my tag as the "digital guy" as technologies were exponentially expanding, opening worlds of opportunity for brands. However, I was still struggling to get a seat at the business planning table for many client organizations to truly drive the business forward leveraging this technological boom. This is when we entered the world of "always on" connectivity with the adoption of smartphones. At this point in my career, I was working at VMLY&R and building the foundational infrastructure for social, mobile and innovation Centers of Excellence for global brands like Colgate-Palmolive, Hershey's, Tom's of Maine and SAP. The acceptance and adoption of doing things differently, although not fully embraced, had started to reverberate throughout the halls of these large, global organizations. The development of these Centers of Excellence created the capability of actually hearing and listening to the voice of the customer on an individual level, at scale. It also provided the ability to take that insight to better communicate with these individuals on the smartphones that were now found in every pocket and purse. Harnessing this transformation gave the brands I worked with the ability to understand what was important to their customers while embarking on a transformational shift of talking *with* their customers, not just *at* them.

Lesson Learned: The voice of the customer is a wealth of information. The ability to connect on an individual level is a massive responsibility for the brand. As these shifts were taking place customer expectations started to gain exponential power in the creation, development, and management of our brands.

Lesson #4: 2012 was the year where "Digital First" was shouted from every boardroom and agency across the globe. It was no different in my career. As the digital lead for

Hudson Rouge, the agency built by WPP for the rebrand of Lincoln, Ford's luxury brand, things were no different. But what struck me as odd about the task was that the request focused on marketing efforts, not necessarily what digital can do for business or brand building. That wouldn't come for another few years. The challenge for Lincoln, specifically, was attracting a new customer type to revive the brand and solidify a future pipeline of customers as new vehicles were launched. To do this, we knew we had to not only make big splashes in the marketplace just to get noticed, but also take that initial interaction and turn it into an ongoing relationship, ready to take the next step when the time is right. So, we embarked on creating an organization that moved beyond a campaign mindset toward developing an always-on relationship with customers. We knew that we couldn't oversell our new target audience and that they wouldn't be ready to buy in a moment's notice. But we also knew we had to deliver demand and sales of vehicles on the ground today. So, we had to balance our efforts to provide the right content and call to action at the right moment based on the customer's behavioral triggers. We developed big, immersive experiences that drew great news and headlines while engaging a highly targeted marketing machine that used customer data, conversational content and transaction models to deliver messaging sequences based on previous interactions or customer expectations. This is how we ultimately defined "Digital First"—providing content and interaction "Just in time, not just in case;" delivering results in the short-term while building the brand over the long-term.

Lesson Learned: Digital First isn't a media mix. It's a fundamental transformation in how we interact with customers and nurture them through a relationship on their terms.

Lesson #5: In 2016–2017 there was an onslaught of disruption taking place for many companies. The rise of digital businesses like Uber, Airbnb and Tesla were fundamentally transforming the value propositions of entire industries. All without the legacy business models and overhead needed to compete in the manufacturing world of the past. These disruptions went beyond marketing a product and transformed the challenge of an organization to provide an integrated customer experience. Value propositions went from more, more, more to simplified problem-solving, tackling one pain point at a time. Learning from the lessons of the first dotcom bubble, these disruptors embraced a new way of working to continuously find and create product-market fit, while building new value along the way by listening to and responding to their customer and market needs. While winding down my tenure at Hudson Rouge working with Lincoln, we were faced with solving a simple challenge—"Our industry is moving from manufacturing to mobility and from ownership to membership, how do we plan for this for our brand and our business?" To solve this, we embarked on a strategic quest to define a ten-year roadmap that defined the future of the brand, product, and the experiences that surrounded it. We looked at customer expectations and data, industry trends, product evolution, mobility behaviors and the sentiment around personal transportation to get from Point A to Point B and the multi-modal world in which some folks lived. The outcome was to align the entire customer supply chain to create new and incremental value from removing pain points or optimizing moments of joy. We developed digital tools to connect the owner to the product, their service and their relationship to the brand. We developed service programs that took away challenging moments of ownership, like personalized maintenance and on-demand service. And we integrated mobility tools like parking and refueling into the experience to help solve challenges of transportation. All in all, we leveraged technology and data to craft new business models, new customer engagement moments and new value propositions throughout the entirety of the customer experience and relationship.

Lesson Learned: Digital enables the brand and the business of the future. It's never technology for technology's sake but what technology can create when coupled with a robust brand strategy and the right product, service and business model.

TODAY AND TOMORROW

Looking back, it's been a fast twenty years. The lessons learned are all coming to a head in a paradigm shift of epic proportions for our businesses, our customers and the environment in which our brands have to capture, create and fulfill value. Tomorrow will be no different. And, with the continued advances in technology and pace of disruption, this change is becoming exponential. In fact, during the first three months of the COVID-19 Pandemic in 2020, McKinsey reported that we experienced ten years of growth in e-commerce penetration, leaving those businesses that were prepared for the inevitable transformation reaping massive rewards while those that weren't lost out or eventually had to shutter.

Ultimately, we've reached a point in history where it's not if and when you should do something but it's if you don't do something, you die.

When talking about digital transformation or customer

experience, I've heard businesses call it modern marketing, customer value creation, new business model development, disruption, innovation, etc. However, what I've noticed is that many larger, lagging organizations are looking for that silver bullet to leapfrog their competition with the majority thinking they don't have to do the leg work of the last twenty years to succeed. The issue here, of course, is that there are table stakes that need to be developed in order to succeed in this paradigm shifting Journey Economy. The lessons learned above bring with them the opportunity of tomorrow. Only by establishing a progressive strategy based on insight and consumer expectations, enabled with technology, will you have the elements for future success.

At the start of my career, I tried desperately not to be pigeonholed into being the tech guy or the digital guy. But looking back, I see that hole is exactly where we all need to be. Using a backbone of digital theory, connectivity and processes, we can look at our business challenges and brand opportunities from a systems perspective rather than a linear mindset. This mindset shift opens a world of opportunity to better connect with and create value for our customers all while creating value for our brands. This is the real paradigm shift.

ABOUT THIS BOOK

This book is all about action. The action that will allow you, your business and your brands to harness the power of the paradigm shifts of today and prepare you to capitalize on the unforeseen opportunities of tomorrow. By understanding the nuance of the external factors influencing the business environment, the changing consumer and the accelerated pace of technology, you will be able to identify and define new opportunities for your brand and business. You will understand the transformation toward the Journey Economy where moments of value go way beyond a simple purchase transaction created by an advertised message and into a personalized journey that meets your customers with a simplified experience brought to them on their terms in a way that only your brand can. You will be able to establish your brand as an Experience Brand, something that intentionally creates the experience journey the customer goes through to do business with you, finding ways to fulfill your brand promise along the way. You will create the building blocks for customer-centric brand development from go-to-market, to commerce, to membership, and into business model development. Finally, you will know how your organization must transform to implement your Experience Brand strategy.

This book is not a guide for a reorganization but a vision for a new organization for you and your brand. One that charts its own course and fulfills its own destiny by creating the best ongoing experience possible for its customers. Built from on-the-ground experiences, customer behaviors and digital transformation, you will have the knowledge to prepare your organization to be future ready, whatever that requires.

The book is broken into four sections to provide an organic structure to identify the challenges, create new strategies, execute and implement the solutions at scale. This structure gives you the power and insight to progress your brand strategy from insight to implementation, bringing success today and in the future.

Part 1 Insight: The Journey Economy

Part 2 Idea: The Experience Brand

Part 3 Execution: The Growth Action Plan

Part 4 Implementation: The Operating Model

The chapter structure will give you the tools and insights needed to help you build your Experience Brand. With each chapter building on the one before it, you will have a step-by-step action plan to define, establish, execute and implement your Experience Brand strategy. As we'll see, there is a new way of working to succeed in the Journey Economy. Following the established and proven process laid out in the following pages will guide you through new and continued brand growth.

Resource Guide

To accompany this book, the strategies discussed, and the technologies and platforms needed to succeed, I've created an interactive resource guide in the appendix of this book and at www.JourneyEconomy.com. This guide is meant to give you the tools needed to facilitate, implement and execute your Experience Brand strategy across your organization.

 I will refer to the Resource Guide throughout the book to accommodate any real-life examples or strategic models.

www.JourneyEconomy.com/

Ask the Author

I want to give you the ability to ask me questions as you're going through your own learning and exploration of the content. Feel free to drop me a question at any time, even if it's outside of the realm of the chapter information. I'll do the best

 I can to answer on Twitter or through accompanying content. Simply use the hashtag and my handle and I'll respond.

#ExperienceBrand@PaulMiser

PART I

INSIGHT

The Journey Economy

"It is not necessary to change. Survival is not mandatory."

W. Edwards Deming

CHAPTER 1

THE WINDS OF CHANGE

Where Are We, Really?

"To know the laws that govern the winds, and to know that you know them, will give you an easy mind . . .; otherwise you may tremble at the appearance of every cloud."

Joshua Slocum

WHEN sailing, the captain of a ship can never rest, for the wind will never rest. To chart a course and keep the right heading, the captain must always be watching for clues in the wind to give her the insight to adjust the sails and tack accordingly. The wind, as simple as it sounds, can make or break a captain. It can turn a leisurely sail into a tumultuous experience. Its power is in its uncertainty. The thing about wind is that there are many variables that can influence it or cause it to change. But, at its very core, wind is change. This change can be as little as an offshore breeze reflecting off a cliff or as big as a squall forming in the distance, forcing the captain to always be aware and alert. But what the sailor watches most of all is the strength that comes along with the wind. As the wind speed increases, the force or pressure of that wind increases exponentially not directly. So, thinking a wind increase from five to ten miles per hour packs twice the punch is wrong. In reality, doubling the wind speed quadruples the force of the wind. Understanding these dynamics and weathering the uncertain winds is what makes a great sailor. Without the challenging winds, the sailor would never be forced to learn, grow and evolve. And on the seas, the only lessons to learn is through these experiences.

As the wind is harnessed change for the sailor, the varying external factors in a business environment is for the business leader. There are many different forces that are continuously creating areas of change for a business that a leader must successfully navigate through or around to find growth for their brands. Each force creates its own set of challenges and opportunities but, combined with other forces, can create brand new environments or industries to chart and navigate. As we've seen in the last five years, only to be accelerated through the COVID-19 Pandemic, increased pressure against these external forces in the business environment are creating exponential change for many businesses and entire industries. This has created a situation for business leaders to either rise to the occasion and harness these winds of change or lose control of their ship or, at worst, sink it.

Like any good sailor, understanding the charts and how to use the wind, business leaders proving successful in this time of transformation are succeeding by adjusting accordingly and capitalizing on opportunities as they arise. To do this ourselves, we must first understand the external and internal forces that are creating these winds of change to best build a navigational plan—one that will work for our individual businesses and brands.

EXTERNAL FACTORS

Let's start with the macroeconomic trends that are affecting almost every organization in some way—some harder than others. These macro-trend forces have been growing over the last ten years, but, as we'll explore, they have accelerated in the last five years, hitting their tipping point in 2020. These macro trends are creating a challenging situation for established brands to find true, sustained growth as it requires change to do so. Whether you are navigating changing trade issues within your supply chain, fending off new market entrants, trying to stay ahead of the changing consumer mindset, or just looking for new ways to generate growth, you're more than likely scratching your head over what to do next. However, as we'll quickly see, the overarching problem we are facing is that we're five years into a new economy and have yet to upgrade our growth mindset and action plan to succeed with the changing times.

Political and Economic Risk

The first macro trend, Political and Economic Risk, needs no introduction, as we are all living it each and every day.

Confidence in economic growth is declining due to several factors. In 2020, the U.S. economy declined a minus 3.5 percent GDP growth, with 2021 projected only to recap the pandemic economic retraction. This environment where growth is really only getting back to parity is a challenge for business leaders.

The Conference Board Base Case Economic Outlook, 2019-2020-2021

Percentage Change, Seasonally Adjusted Annual Rates

	2019	2020	2021
	ANNUAL	ANNUAL	ANNUAL
Real GDP	2.2	-3.5	3.5
Real Consumer Spending	2.4	-4.4	4.0

To cap off the sluggish and poor growth projections, Global CEO growth confidence fell 15 percent from 2019-2021, moving from confident to cautiously optimistic. As such, more than one third of CEOs are planning to make workforce and sizeable capital spending reductions over the next year.

Industry optimism follows consistently with the overarching view of the business environment. Another key factor playing into this decline is geo-political uncertainty which brings economic uncertainty. According to KPMG, 52 percent of CEOs believe the political landscape has had a greater impact on their organization than they have seen in many years. Thirty-one percent believe there will be an increase in protectionist policies in their country over the next three years, continuing to create challenge and uncertainty for organizations and growth.

The Cycles Driving The World

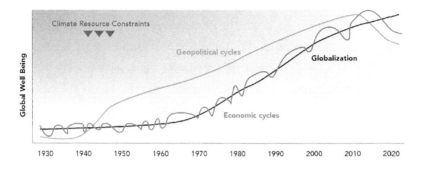

Political Risk Monitor – Source: Eurasia Group
https://www.eurasiagroup.net/files/upload/top_risks_2020_coronavirus_edition_1.pdf

An analysis of The Political Risk Monitor from the Eurasia Group showcases the political risk, based on sentiment over time. Across the globe, there is not only a declining sentiment in political risk but also a steady uneasiness in the general global economy.

This insight is used by business leaders to manage spending risks, to know where to invest their resources, or decide how to capture investment opportunities in new markets.

Even with these geo-political and economic risks, the number-one strategic priority for CEOs (53%) is increasing the penetration in established markets. These CEOs looking to drive growth will not only have to overcome these challenges, but also create growth through products that are fit for new regions and markets—putting increased pressure and responsibility on the product, service, and overarching experience. As we'll see in the changing consumer trend, launching in a new market isn't as simple as providing the same product to a new audience. Rather, it is increasingly becoming a more personalized approach to the value proposition for the market needs and expectations.

Competitive Disruption

Disruption has become a conduit for market transformation and has started to create a chasm between those who disrupt and those who don't. The business leaders who embrace technology, innovation, and consumer centricity are the ones who are not only capturing current market value for brand growth, but also are changing the dynamics of their industries, markets, or sectors to create new value in the marketplace.

Technological advances in almost every aspect of business has drastically changed the competitive set. It's reducing the barriers to entry, increasing the sheer number of competitors in an industry coming in as Disruptive Insurgents. It's also changing how incumbents are coming to market through product, service and experience development—transforming themselves into "Reinvented" Incumbents. These factors are creating increased options and choice for consumers, putting strain and stress on a company's traditional value proposition and offerings.

McKinsey released a report in early 2019 showing the transformation of growth created by digital business. Most of the

Revenue & Profit Growth
From Digital

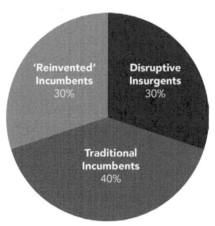

Mckinsey Growth – Source Mckinsey - https://www.mckinsey.com/business-functions/ mckinsey-digital/our-insights/five-fifty-the-legacy-threat

growth from digital in any given industry is being eroded by Disruptive Insurgents and "Reinvented Incumbents," leaving only 40 percent of the pie for traditional incumbents to capture—and that percentage is diminishing quickly.

Not only are these technology-driven businesses and value propositions eroding market share, they're actually performing better as a business. In the McKinsey study, "Reinvented Incumbents" generated two-and-a-half times better revenue growth, two times better EBIT and two times better ROI on digital over their traditional incumbent counterparts— proving that being more digital makes an organization more attractive, more efficient and more effective.

According to KPMG, only 65 percent of CEOs see disruption as an opportunity and only 74 percent say they want to find growth by creating disruption. By leveraging technology, disruptive CEOs are charting a course for new business models and creating new ways to understand and engage consumers. As we saw from the Political and Economic risk, with the estimated U.S. economic growth rate of minus 4.9 percent, the only way to grow is for business leaders to find new ways to intentionally *create* growth. *Capturing* the growth available in most industries is no longer an option. Innovation and disruption are crucial to creating and finding this new value.

Changing Consumer

In their 1999 book *The Experience Economy*, B. Joseph Pine II and James H. Gilmore illustrate the, then, transformation of industry from product and service and into "experiences." They attribute the shift to the ongoing rise of consumer expectations as industry products and services become commoditized after exposure, engagement, and consumption. Using Starbucks as the poster child of the Experience Economy, the authors communicate the symbiotic value exchange between brand and consumer when experiences are offered—consumers paying a premium on coffee in exchange for a new coffee-drinking experience.

Now, fast-forward twenty years and layer on the technological advances of mobile, big data, and social media, and we are living in an always-on, connected, and personalized experience economy. All of these factors have contributed to the rise in value expectations consumers have from the brands they do business with. This rise in consumer expectations has been evolving faster and faster as consumers engage with new value propositions and offerings across most industries.

These expectations are now being established at the second or third level of influence, meaning the experience a consumer has in one industry directly affects the expectations they have in another. For example, the ease of accessing an Uber has a direct experience expectation that consumers have with their dry cleaners. These expectations are forcing brands and businesses to create and deliver offerings beyond product and service—into experience. According to a Walker study, consumers will use a brand's consumer experience as their number-one driver for their purchase decision—surpassing both product efficacy and even price as their determining factor.

Stalling Industries

Looking at each of the above problems, we can clearly see the transformation of many industries—each contributing toward the paradigm shift in a company's value creation and growth prospects. The summation of these trends is forcing many industries into stalling or declining growth periods, furthering the strain on the business leaders in these industries. According to the S&P Ratings, the average cross-industry growth rate for 2019 was a mere 4 percent collectively. Couple that with the 2020 U.S. economic growth-rate decline of minus 3.5 percent and we see organizations competing for an organic growth rate that is leveling off or declining, meaning it is no longer viable for a company to base its growth targets on industry growth alone. They must find a new way to win.

Stalling Industry—S&P Global Rankings

Estimated global non-financial sector revenue growth and EBITDA margin change in 2019

Source: S&P Global Ratings

Revenue Growth (2019 YOY %)

Difference in EBITDA Margin, 2018-2019 (%)

Growth in tomorrow's business environment will look much different than it does today. As we've seen, competition will become fiercer, consumer expectations will continue to exponentially shift, and technology will continue to transform behaviors—all changing the value brands must create. Looking at disruptive models and offerings outside of your current focus will give your brand the insights into where to find growth opportunities.

As we'll explore later, the new brand growth action plan will become a combination of conquering competition, market share management, adjacent-market entry, and increased value exchange for the consumer through experience.

INTERNAL FACTORS

The next set of factors inhibiting growth is our business itself. For years, we've built our businesses and organizations to add new things like financing, warranties, and maintenance to our core offering to try to drive new revenue from a business point of view. Rarely, have we looked at our core offerings from a consumer's perspective to see how we can best serve them.

This business-first minded expansion has created disjointed business units, splintered goals and objectives, disconnected processes, and scattered talent within the organization. Not to mention the havoc it creates for the consumer's experience with unnecessary hoops to jump through just to do business with our brands. It's no wonder consumers are longing for a better experience from the brands they do business with. These internal factors are literally debilitating our prospects for growth by creating unnecessary bureaucracy, slowing decision making and stopping innovation.

Silos

Traditionally, organizational structures have been built around key processes or metrics. These structures have established business-unit silos within the organization with each focused on their own, disparate goals and objectives. Marketing departments have different goals than sales and service, than financing, than brand teams, etc. These silos were built for efficiency and focus in the past business and brand environments but have become inhibitors to growth in today's new, fast-paced economy. The internal silos create fragmented communication and fragmented experiences for the consumer, breaking their holistic relationship with the brand. Silos in an organization create pain points for consumers. These pain points become ripe for disruption.

Legacy

Working with some of the largest, most respected companies throughout my career, it's amazing to see the levels of legacy that permeate organizations. Legacy processes. Legacy technology. Legacy operating structures. Legacy thinking. Legacy becomes the rust on a ship. It slowly corrodes the efficacy of the organization by holding back innovation, thinking, and change, all of which is needed to continue to add value to consumers and intentionally create growth. Establishing new mindsets, implementing new technologies, and optimizing operational processes is the core of the transformation needed to find and create growth.

Talent

Let's face it, we live in a technology-driven, digital-first world. Our customers are highly connected, our processes are enabled by technology and data. The companies that best harness this power get to market quickly, automate experiences, and connect on a deeper level with their customers. These facts create the need for a different type of talent. Breaking down silos and blasting through legacy requires a different mindset and a different set of skills for an organization. The best companies are taking the time to understand this need and upskill or reskill talent to support their transformations for success today, while preparing for tomorrow.

LIVING UP TO YOUR POTENTIAL

Facing both the external forces creating the winds of change and the stifling internal structures of our organizations, we're often blind to the possibilities our brands actually have with our customers. Instead of seeing the full potential of what we could and should be, we continuously feel the noose tightening and gears slowly rusting as we set our course toward a lackluster growth created by industry or external factors. A key theme throughout this book is to help you, not only define the potential your brand has with your customers, but to unleash that potential through a new mindset and toolbox to both capture and create new value. It starts with breaking the constrained mindset of status quo.

Looking across industry sectors, we see some frightening statistics as it relates to growth even before the COVID-19 Pandemic. Retail was only growing at 2 percent; Financial services at 1.1 percent; Apparel at 0.3 percent and Auto at 0.2 percent to name a few industries. These growth rates, if you can call it growth, have become the standard on which we base our own company's growth targets—vying for a piece of an ever-shrinking pie of total industry growth. If we follow this trend year over year for too many years, we are creating a recipe for disaster.

By operating at the industry status quo mindset, we keep our organizations out of the realm of creativity and possibility. We get caught up in the idea of legacy, "we've always done it this way" mindsets, and the paralysis of short-term versus long-term thinking. By changing perspectives, targets, incentives, and strategies, companies can not only define what their potential could be but chart a course to realize it.

The good news is there is something truly extraordinary happening. As the winds of change bring chaos to those novice sailors, the captains who have prepared for these winds are harnessing the opportunities as they come. Organizations that are finding and creating exponential growth during these tumultuous times have broken down the blinders of status quo and risen to a different realm of possibility. They have gone beyond a mindset of direct competition and have looked internally for insight and opportunity. By truly understanding their customers' needs and the dynamics of their behaviors, these Growth Brands are connecting need with value created at the most basic levels of their organizations. They see and do things differently, as if they are operating in a completely different economy.

THE JOURNEY ECONOMY

This new economy is not like the traditional one many organizations are built to participate in. It's not one where our brands grow by simply creating a product or service and then advertising it to the masses, nor is it one where the companies with the biggest media spend wins. Rather, it is one where growth is created by the brands that intimately and continuously understand and exceed their consumer's expectations. An economy where value is both captured and created throughout the entirety of the consumer journey— from the product to the service surrounding it; from the customer support to the delivery of the product; from the initial moment of awareness to the ongoing ownership relationship. It's built not from a singular view of a product or service, but as a collection and summation of all things throughout the supply chain from sourcing to marketing to membership to logistics. Each of these moments of opportunity are giving Growth Brands the ability to bring their brand strategy to life in new ways, ushering in a new echelon of brand-value proposition beyond product and service and into experience and personalization.

This is the Journey Economy.

As we'll see in the next chapter, there is a spectrum of Growth Brands that are harnessing the winds of the Journey

Economy to not only meet and exceed their consumers' expectations but to fulfill their brand strategy, living up to their full potential. As brands find new ways to create value propositions throughout the entire consumer journey, they find new opportunities to drive economic value—increased revenue, increased efficiencies, new revenue, recurring revenue, and expanded offerings beyond products or services. The Journey Economy, although different, opens opportunity and gives power to your brand to be intentional in creating growth, rather than accepting the fate of the status quo industry growth rates provide. By establishing a new Journey Economy strategy, your brand can and will expand to achieve its full potential.

WRAPPING UP

After a nascent decade, and then accelerating drastically during the COVID-19 Pandemic, the paradigm shift of the Journey Economy is creating havoc in boardrooms across the world. With the trends of increasing economic and political risk, growing competitive disruption, continually changing consumers, and stalling industry growth, brands are seeing their traditional strategies and action plans becoming ineffective and obsolete. As technology continues to evolve and consumer behaviors and expectations transform, these trends aren't going away anytime soon. In fact, we'll see them grow exponentially in the coming years, bringing urgency to the transformation of brand value, and in turn, the brand experience.

The core of our organizational development is on the verge of transformation. Not only are organizational structures and processes in need of an overhaul to create a more seamless and consistent value exchange with consumers, but also the very definition of the potential growth and market positioning needs to be reexamined. Companies that base their growth expectations on industry or competitive benchmarks will maintain the status quo that is becoming the detriment for many brands across many industries. Only through shifting mindset and organizational structure, will brands have the ability to transform their fate.

The good news is that there are companies that have been able to find and create growth within these shifting and growing challenges. The purpose of this book and the following chapters is to understand how growth is being created, what these companies are doing differently to create growth, and what are the strategies and best practices to learn from. My goal is to help you transform your mindset and give you the tools to succeed in this ever-changing business environment.

www.JourneyEconomy.com/chapter-1

#change@PaulMiser

LESSONS LEARNED

- Challenges for brand growth exist externally as well as internally. All brands in an industry are facing the same external macro trend challenges (political and economic uncertainty, competitive disruption, changing consumer values and expectation, and stalling growth). It's the internal challenges that define the ability for a brand to create growth.

- Consumer behaviors and expectations have drastically changed in the last five years and are on pace to compound changes in the next five. Brands can only find growth by meeting and exceeding these expectations today and as they evolve.

- The way organizations are structured and how they currently operate is magnifying market challenges across the organization. Working in silos creates broken communication internally and broken relationships with consumers externally.

- Aiming for market growth rates doesn't create growth. It inhibits growth. Only brands that plan beyond market rates by finding and calculating their potential have the urgency and need to transform to find growth.

- The Journey Economy is emerging as a way brands can intentionally create growth while building new value throughout the entirety of the consumer journey.

CHAPTER 2

ENTERING THE JOURNEY ECONOMY

"Victory comes from finding opportunities in problems."

Sun Tzu

WHILE in business school in the early 2000s, I was required to read a book that would become the foundation of my point of view throughout my career. As mentioned earlier *The Experience Economy* by B. Joseph Pine II and James H. Gilmore was an eye-opening read that took brands beyond the commodification of products and services and into something more. Something consumers could subscribe to be a part of. Something that could be a defining element of a consumer's life. Something that aspired to be more. An experience. This idea of the Experience Economy was written in 1999 using Starbucks as the poster child, providing value beyond coffee as s drink and into a physical, engaging experience of cool with coffee as the hero.

Now fast-forward twenty years and add in the evolution of technology (smartphones, social media, data, Internet of Things and the like) along with the continued rising consumer expectations and we, as brands, are facing a new economy in which we have to build brands and create value. This is the Journey Economy—where value isn't just a singular trans-action in a moment in time but a progressive collection of moments and interactions that capture and create value over the entirety of the consumer experience journey and relation-ship. As such, these technological advances and rising expec-tations have changed the process of staging experiences. It has moved beyond the physical with a one-and-done moment, like the Starbucks example in *The Experience Economy* and into a progressive experience that blends the digital with the physical and connects the consumer's expectations and needs with a brand's promise over the entire course of the relation-ship between brand and consumer. Staging experiences has become more of a connected, personalized story arc of com-munication and interaction over time than just a cool place to go have coffee. As these multi-touchpoint, progressive, staged experiences come to life, consumers are looking for the brands that are removing the pain points of traditional industries as well as celebrating moments of joy that are created through-out the path of interaction, purchase and ownership.

This massive paradigm shift has created a new competitive environment in which our brands must participate and shine. By leveraging all assets a brand has at its disposal—physical, digital, human and data—brands create new value propositions that are transforming industries each and every day. Not only are they finding new ways to deliver traditional products and services but are making entire companies around the biggest pain points in certain industries. Uber is built around the pain point of hailing a cab, Casper was built around the pain point of shopping for a mattress, Smile Direct Club was built around the pain point of getting braces through an orthodontist. In effect, the Journey Economy is upending the entire idea of value in many industries, forever changing how brands compete. It's an economy where a new disruptor can gain fast followings and capture market share; where the consumer purchase decision is driven by the experience and fulfilled by the product or service; where continuous innovation and transformation is the new barrier to entry; where brands build true, lasting relationships with their consumers through ongoing engagement and continuous trust, all producing a situation where conventional brand growth is getting harder and harder to come by. And, in effect, is proving our traditional growth action plans ineffective.

THE JOURNEY ECONOMY

To better understand the winds of change and the paradigm shift of the Journey Economy, I set out to see around the corners of growth, to identify the new strategies, approaches and actions brands are taking to fully live their brand and achieve their potential. I embarked on finding those companies that were breaking the mold and achieving noticeable, sustained growth. Not just any growth, but step-change, innovative growth that has broken the barriers of the norm, setting new trends in consumer expectations, value propositions, and scale. I was eager to find the heroes of the moment; the white spaces in the world of business; the brands that, despite all challenges facing them, manage to create and scale growth. I wanted to learn from the best to understand the trends and strategies and operating models that drive this exponential growth for us all to learn from.

To find these brands, I developed a study to map areas of growth across industry. I created a Fortune 500 cohort as a control group for growth to have a benchmark to measure against. Again, I wanted to find the step-change innovative growth; the companies that were breaking the barriers of the status quo as it related to industry growth trends and then deconstructing the strategies to build a new brand growth action plan. With the control group in place, I measured growth rates, both public and private, across industry to identify the individual and groups of companies that were breaking the mold against the control group. The metrics that were used to uncover the Growth Brand segments were:

- **Growth Rates:** Framed at Year-on-Year growth rates by revenue and EBITDA to illustrate true, efficient growth.

- **Value Proposition:** Its customer base and the revenue opportunities this creates.

- **Brand Strength:** The brand value over time—consistency and strength of the message and simplicity in brand value.

- **Innovation:** Timing and implementation of new products, services, or experiences that increase value to the consumer relationship.

These metrics generated both leading and lagging insights that would not only show how these Growth Brands did things differently to find current success but also how they were preparing for future success. The result would showcase the actions and differences in their approach to truly find growth in today's Journey Economy.

What I found were three distinct groups of brands doing things differently; looking at challenges with a new perspective, approaching the marketplace with new strategies and value propositions, and creating new revenue opportunities for their organizations. I call these the "Growth Brands." These Growth Brands were then classified into three distinct groups: "Trillion Dollar Brands," "Unicorns," and "Transformational Brands."

Let's take a deeper look at these Growth Brand segments and why they were selected to explore, contextualize, and learn from.

TRILLION DOLLAR BRANDS

In late 2018, the business community witnessed a historical race to the Trillion Dollar Market Capitalization Valuation. For the first time in history, a company would be valued at over $1 Trillion. The companies in the running were Alphabet, Amazon, Apple, and Microsoft with Apple winning the race. However, Amazon and Microsoft would tip over the mark months later and finally Alphabet crossed the line. And, during the writing of this book in mid-2020, Apple added another $1 Trillion to its market valuation, making it the first company to hit $2 Trillion in market valuation. This historic event was loaded with lessons and learnings that I couldn't wait to dive into. However, going into the study, I wanted to avoid technology companies as the valuations were based on different metrics than traditional Fortune 500 companies. But upon further examination, each Trillion Dollar Brand is made up of a collection of physical products, services and, what we'll see later, experiences—truly capitalizing on the opportunities provided in the Journey Economy. Each part of that collection adds to the revenue streams and overall value proposition that other brands can and should learn from. Technology was a component, but wasn't necessarily the be all, end all of these organizations. Not to mention, many traditional industry leaders have started classifying themselves as *"Technology companies that do (X)."* So, if the traditional playing field was transitioning toward leading as a technology company, then these Trillion Dollar Brands should become a model for all to learn from.

Alphabet

With a portfolio of companies ranging from Google Search to Google Ventures to Google Next, Alphabet provides a data connected ecosystem of home products, information technology, and business services. Its revenue model is multifold, from advertising to product sales to subscription models, providing the right value for their customers in the right context.

Amazon

Amazon, traditionally known for the e-commerce retail marketplace, also provides physical products like Kindle, Fire, Alexa and business offerings like Amazon Web Services (AWS). All add to the bottom line for the growth and valuation of Amazon. Their innovations in subscription services like Amazon Prime and logistics has changed the way customers shop forever.

Apple

At its core, Apple is a device manufacturer of smartphones, computers, and watches. With the implementation of services like iTunes, the App Store, and experiences like Apple TV+, Apple News, and Apple Wallet, Apple has established a network of revenue-generating offerings. Apple has become almost an operating system for the lives of their customers, with value captured and created in the right moments to build revenue beyond products and subscriptions.

Microsoft

As a software giant, Microsoft has pivoted over the last few years to offer increased products, services, and recurring experiences. From Office to Azure to Xbox to Surface, Microsoft has expanded its value proposition for its various consumer types. Microsoft, riding the SaaS (software as a service) model of subscription pricing has drastically changed its relationships with its customers.

UNICORN BRANDS

With over 600 Unicorns (privately held companies valued over $1 billion) in the world in 2020, we can surmise that something powerful is happening in the business world. However, we could easily dismiss the entire concept of Unicorns as a Growth Brand Segment as the idea of Unicorns has been in hot water recently with runaway valuations and not ideal management practices—harkening back to the dotcom bubble of the late 90s and early 2000s. But there is something to be learned in the fast-growing startup space. These companies not only found value to be created in the market but had the wherewithal and staying power to capture interest, revenue and market share in a short period of time. As such, they intentionally created new value in the market. When looking for companies that fit my criteria and are experiencing step-change growth, I found some interesting movement happening in extremely traditional or saturated industries. The 'Unicorn' brand group is illustrated by the companies that have not only changed the value proposition in their category but also have affected the consumer behaviors within those categories, captured industry market share, and have an aligned market value, coming to their value proposition. These 'Unicorns' found pain points in stagnating industries; then they set out to solve for specific needs while expanding their relationships with their customers on an individual level.

Glossier

What started as a blog has turned into a coveted brand for beauty products and experiences. The value they create is a combination of service, products, information, and retail/pop up experiences. With influencer partnerships and new product launches, Glossier has continued to grow their consumer base that nearly doubled its revenue from 2018 to 2020.

Airbnb

Disrupting one of the most walled-off industries is no easy feat. But Airbnb has been able to gain traction in its dual-sided economy of house rentals, while expanding their value into local and city experiences. It has massively increased its growth over the last couple of years with a staggering 21-percent year-on-year growth in 2019. This growth has been created by expanding into new markets and launching new products, services and experiences.

Sweetgreen

Not only does Sweetgreen tap into the trend of healthy, organic, fast-casual dining, but it has increased its value through the experience its consumers have with their brand —from VIP delivery to corporate partnerships, to sustainability in packaging and product. Its growth has been focused on generating repeat clientele and capitalizing on opportunities in its target locations.

Smile Direct Club

Smile Direct Club has taken a tortuous process of straightening teeth and made it accessible and easy. Its value isn't necessarily in its end output, but in the process and experience to get there, bringing the process to the consumer. Its growth has been steadily outpacing analyst projections, forcing the company to incorporate a "controlled growth" strategy to ensure a long-term view for the brand.

Warby Parker

In a category dominated by one major player, Warby Parker has found a value that has started to disrupt. Leading with product and pricing innovation, Warby Parker has expanded its value through innovations in trial, preparation, purchase, and retail for eyewear—expanding beyond the product and into services.

TRANSFORMATIONAL BRANDS

As we saw in the McKinsey study in Chapter 1, there is a segment of traditional incumbent brands and companies that have embraced digital opportunities to transform their brands and value in the marketplace. McKinsey called these brands "Reinvented Incumbents." However, I don't feel that truly captures the enormity of what these brands have accomplished in their organization and in the market. For our purposes, we'll call this Growth Brand segment, Transformational Brands. To truly embrace the paradigm shift of digital and all that it offers for businesses and customers, brands have to completely transform who they are and what they do. These companies have studied the consumer behavior and technological shifts happening in their respective direct and adjacent industries to change the way their business operates and the end value they create for their consumers and brands. This Growth Brand segment covers various sizes of mid-market all the way to Fortune 10 organizations.

Walmart

Walmart has been making interesting advances for a few years to help it transform from a brick and mortar retailer and into a digital-driven organization that adds new value to its consumer relationships. With the acquisition of Bonobos and Jet.com, Walmart has been acquiring the talent and infrastructure to harness the winds of change in the retail category.

Ford

Ford has begun its transformation toward a transportation and mobility company over the last few years. After the launch of FordPass, its mobility program and consumer app, it has been making drastic updates to its technology infrastructure build toward its future of an organization. By implementing over-air updates to vehicles, consumer connectivity to its vehicles and dealers and enhancements to the electrification of their vehicles, Ford is building the foundation for incremental and new relationships and experiences with its customers.

Marriott

With disruption in the hospitality industry from companies like Airbnb, Marriott has transformed into an experiential leader. From content to new properties to a network of individual homes, Marriott has built the assets needed to create new value for its guests. Layer on the investment it has made to its loyalty and rewards program, Bonvoy, and you have the recipe for massive growth in the long term.

GROWTH BRAND FINDINGS

Throughout the research process, I documented the similarities among the three Growth Brand groups and then mapped them against the Fortune 500 cohort. What was interesting was that the similarities among Trillion Dollar Brands, Unicorns and Transformational Brands were more aligned than not. These business, organizational and communication trends could then be used as a foundation for a new brand growth strategy. As we'll see throughout the rest of this chapter, these Growth Brand characteristics surrounded all aspects of business—how they approached their businesses, how they thought about growth, and the actions they took to create growth. There seemed to be an intentional, curious and continuously evolving approach to value capture and, more importantly, creation—focusing on both their core businesses while expanding into new avenues and pathways of value and revenue.

The four most significant characteristics for growth creation of the Growth Brand segments are:

- Perspective and Mindset
- Fulfillment of the Brand Promise
- Developing a Holistic Experience
- Enabled by Technology

PERSPECTIVE & MINDSET

The first and most prevalent characteristic identified was the perspective and mindset the Growth Brands instilled across their organizations. They were almost obsessed with value creation for the organization and for their customers —continuously pursuing new ideas, new opportunities, and stronger relationships. Where other companies see problems, Growth Brands see opportunity. Where others strive for incrementality, they push for innovation.

Value creation throughout a Growth Brand is made up of making the right decisions; having the right processes, systems, and frameworks in place, garnering the right insight, establishing the right teams, providing the freedom and latitude to test, fail or scale, and continuously looking for new problems and solutions. This Growth Brand mindset is made up of four points of view.

People Obsession

From consumers to employees to stakeholders, Growth Brands are obsessed with people. They look for the true problems facing their different groups and set out to solve them through user experience, consumer experience, or value creation. They understand that the true success is by owning the details of these problems then solving them in the way that only their brand can.

Systems Thinking

Growth Brands don't think linearly; rather they view the world with a filter of systems and frameworks that can be replicated across the organization and through their relationships with their consumers. Having a systems-thinking approach allows Growth Brands to systematically drive change in action, process, and behavior. From strategy to execution to relationship development, Growth Brands act within a series of systems and frameworks for decision making and interaction.

Diversified Talent

Growth Brands make a concerted effort to develop and match talent in new ways—connecting diverse backgrounds with diverse experiences. They understand that the right amount of complimentary and differing characteristics can make decisions stronger and more dramatic. They also pair talent with the right technologies to empower their people to not only service customers better, but also stay more connected with each other in the organization, creating a stronger sense of ownership for every employee.

Continuous Beta

Growth Brands are continuously learning while solving problems. They've adopted the "infinite game" mindset for their business strategy processes—always looking for ways to either optimize, innovate, or pivot. Each pushes the boundaries in what value looks like for the organization and their customers. However, each evolution and iteration is leading closer and closer to their brand purpose, their North Star.

FULFILLMENT OF THE BRAND PROMISE

The entire idea of "brand" is something that Growth Brands think of differently. Traditionally, brands have established a promise, then communicated that promise through advertising or campaigns to drive product purchase with little thought on what comes along with that purchase journey. Growth Brands, on the other hand, view their brand promise as something that is alive—something that must be fulfilled and evolved with each interaction with their customers. They believe their brand promise is only as strong as the last fulfillment. This leads to a relationship-first or retention mindset where the consumer is an active participant in the development and creation of the brand and its experience versus a passive viewer of a brand message that is never truly fulfilled.

Traditional Brand Communications

With the proliferation of personalized devices and curated information gathering, mass advertising has been losing its effectiveness for years. Not only does a brand need to establish its promise and communicate it effectively, but the resulting action and experience must fulfill that promise. Far too often consumers are wooed by shiny, sexy advertising only to go to a website or into a store to be massively let down by the expectation gap. Mass advertising and campaigns alone will never be able to support this consumer behavior transformation. For example, seeing a commercial for a car company and then visiting their website or going into a dealership is often a massive disconnect between promise and reality.

Growth Brand Fulfillment

The success and growth of a brand is determined by its ability to set a certain expectation through messaging and then fulfill or exceed that expectation with each touchpoint or transaction with the consumer. Doing this provides data and insight to progressively grow and expand the relationship with each customer. This relationship-first mindset has created step-change value for the Trillion Dollar Brands, Unicorns, and Transformational Brands alike. For example, the gap between promise and fulfillment for Uber is extremely small. Its brand promise of "Where to?" is fulfilled millions of times each day by its service value proposition.

DEVELOPING A HOLISTIC EXPERIENCE

The next trend and characteristic of Growth Brands is the intentional development and orchestration of a holistic brand experience for their customers. Putting the consumer at the center of the brand experience, these Growth Brands have been able to build a singular view of that consumer while successfully engaging them throughout the entire journey and relationship—from unawareness through purchase, loyalty, and repurchase.

Intimately understanding the entire consumer journey, Growth Brands can create a singular, orchestrated strategy surrounding the consumer by giving each technology, business unit, or department a role to play in the broader relationship with the customer. Using an algorithmic approach, Growth Brands employ a series of "if this, then that" scenarios when crafting and curating their experience and relationship with their consumers. Growth Brands use a combination of internal and external assets to bring the experience to life.

In contrast, traditional organizations have become siloed in their relationship with their consumers due to the siloed nature of the organization itself—splintering messages, offers, and the brand promise. There is a lack of higher-order strategy that connects the business units together for the value to the consumer.

ENABLED BY TECHNOLOGY

Consciously, "Enabled by Technology" is the final defining characteristic of Growth Brands. From an outsider's perspective, one can argue that technology has been the competitive advantage and driving force of the growth witnessed in the Growth Brand cohorts. However, it is the use of technology to fulfill the brand strategy that gives each of the Growth Brands a true advantage. A Growth Brand's strategic growth framework is built off the relationship-first mindset to best leverage data, platforms, and content to ease the pain points throughout the consumer journey while finding new models and opportunities for revenue.

Growth Brands view technology as a strategic facilitator of bringing their brands to life and enabling stronger consumer relationships. Growth Brands believe that technology is never an end in itself but always a means to fulfill a larger strategy. The acceptance and adoption of new technologies by Growth

Brands far outweighs that of the traditional Fortune 500 cohort. Growth Brands successfully connect their consumers' needs with their brand value by using the right technology.

CONSUMER EXPERIENCE

It's worth calling out, the one thing that was consistent throughout the exploration into Growth Brands was their focus on the consumer experience. Every decision they made and every interaction they created seemed to be planned through the lens of the progressive memory they want their consumers to have and they want to have about their consumers. From a strategy standpoint, consumer experience (CX) should be a driving force for business strategy overall. At its very core, the practice of CX is about identifying and fulfilling the needs of the consumer while orchestrating the entire business and operations around that value exchange. As Pine and Gilmore wrote in *The Experience Economy*, consumer expectations rise with each positive interaction with a brand—with expectations now transferring across industry and business. This means that as a business grows along with its consumer expectations, not only does it have to maintain competitive products or services for its industry to solve the core consumer challenges but must also provide a seamless CX for the consumer throughout their individual journey.

To do this, businesses must document and map out the current state of the consumer's journey to understand their state of mind, expectations, and activity at each point of interaction, then set out to remove or reduce moments of pain or chores and expand or spotlight the moments of joy or cherish. By continually reducing pain points and expanding moments of joy, businesses will create a CX strategy that continuously meets or exceeds their consumer expectations, but also grows their business through reduced costs, increased profits, and new revenue opportunities.

With such a focus on consumer experience, let's clarify a few things that will carry on throughout the rest of the book:

What is Consumer Experience (CX)?

Consumer Experience is a brand's intentional creation of the journey and actions a consumer takes to purchase their product, service or brand. From unawareness, through research, shopping, deciding and purchase, through onboarding, service, support, and repurchase, the consumer experience involves all touchpoints, interactions and reactions supporting a consumer's journey with a brand.

This experience ranges from the removal of pain points in the consumption of a product to the business model in which products and services are consumed to the integrated nature of consumption and replenishment.

Why does Consumer Experience Matter?

Providing a positive and powerful consumer experience is good for consumers and good for business. Consumers are expecting a good experience with the brands they buy from. According to a 2018 report from Salesforce:

- 67% of customers say their standard for good experiences are higher than ever, and
- 51% of customers say most companies fall short of their expectations.

Businesses that employ successful consumer experience strategies not only find new ways to grow but they also increase the long-term value of their consumer relationships.

- According to the Temkin Group: a moderate increase in customer experience generates an average revenue increase of $823 million over three years for a company with $1 billion in annual revenues.

What Role does Technology and Data play in Consumer Experience?

As we'll see throughout the book, there is an innate role technology and data plays in bringing Growth Brands to life across the consumer experience. Again, it's never using technology for technology's sake. It's a systematic approach to using technology to fulfill the overarching brand and experience strategy.

Technology and data are used for many different strategic priorities when it comes to providing an ideal experience for consumers.

- It's the data to learn about and target consumers.
- It's the interaction data to progress the consumer relationships forward as they engage with the brand.
- It's the new operations used to remove legacy steps in a process standing in the way of an ideal consumer experience.
- It's the tools or platforms in the form of apps and websites that connect the various players involved in the experience (consumer, employee, retailer, customer service, etc.).
- It's the passive data and information that passes from product to experience, producing an action like a repurchase or reward.
- It's the real-time or aggregate analytics that can be used to optimize an experience or find new value to provide to consumers.

Growth Brands don't view technology as something separate in IT. It is integrated in the strategic decision-making process and is a mindset that each of the brands and their leaders consistently nurture.

THE EXPERIENCE BRAND: OPPORTUNITY IN THE JOURNEY ECONOMY

When layered together, what's wrong with the current business environment is manipulated and capitalized on with the characteristics found in Growth Brands. Gleaning insight from these Growth Brands, we can see a new brand growth strategy and new brand approach emerging to best succeed in the Journey Economy. This evolution is what I call the Experience Brand.

As we'll see in Part II, Experience Brand leaders view their brands and growth differently, with the consumer experience being the driving force for their business decisions. With this mindset, they have the ability not only to see new opportunities but have the insight to react quickly to them as they arise. Experience Brands intentionally create a symbiotic value by connecting what consumers want, with what the brands want from their consumers.

As we'll discuss throughout the book, there is a revolution in how value is captured and created between brands and their consumers. It goes beyond the product, service, or even price, and into the experience a consumer has with your brand. This paradigm shifting value transformation is both global as well as industry specific.

- Value in Auto is no longer the vehicle itself, but the act of getting from Point A to Point B as easily as possible across different modes of transportation.
- Value in Retail is no longer having a storefront, but seamlessly guiding consumers through purchase and service

across devices, screens and aisles—on their terms.

- Value in CPG is no longer a product, but an understanding of consumers' lives to become a trusted advisor who recommends the best products for them.
- Value in Airlines is no longer a seat on an airplane, but an end-to-end travel experience that starts with the planning of a trip and ends while seamlessly integrating into the culture and beat of the destination.
- Value in Manufacturing is no longer a sheet of metal, but a holistic metal solution that can transform the manufacturing experience through interoperability and service.

The opportunity for you and your organization is to move forward from a products or services company and even beyond a technology company that provides products and services. The opportunity, for you, is to transform your brand into an Experience Brand.

Now, let's find out how to do this.

www.JourneyEconomy.com/chapter-2

#shiftingparadigms@PaulMiser

LESSONS LEARNED

- Experience Brands are finding innovative, step-change growth by leveraging the problems outlined in Chapter 1 to build a new approach for brand growth.
- Experience Brands have an organization-wide mindset that differs from traditional Fortune 500 brands. They are People Obsessed (internal and external). They are

Systems Thinkers, meaning their processes are established in scenarios versus linearly. They embrace and expand with Diversified Talent, hiring the right people and putting the right groups together based on data. They are in Continuous Beta, launching, testing and learning along the way.

- Experience Brands perceive their brand as something that is alive. To them their brand promise isn't something that is communicated, but it is something that is fulfilled across each interaction throughout the consumer journey.
- Experience Brands leverage technology as a strategic driver, not as an extension or add-on. They bring technology to the center of the organization and through strategic planning.
- Experience Brands are obsessed with the details in their Consumers' Experience. They intentionally and actively create an experience throughout the entire consumer journey to not only guide the consumer more seamlessly through, but also to find ways to fulfill their brand promise and add new value.
- Experience Brands have the answers and the tools to succeed in the Journey Economy, connecting consumer needs and expectations with new and expanded value propositions. Experience Brands intentionally create and orchestrate the entirety of the consumer experience for traditional and non-traditional growth.

PART 2

IDEA

The Experience Brand

"People do not buy goods and services; they buy relations, stories and magic."

Seth Godin

CHAPTER 3

EXPERIENCE BRAND OVERVIEW

BECOMING AN EXPERIENCE BRAND

"The key is to set realistic customer expectations, and then not to just meet them, but to exceed them—preferably in unexpected and helpful ways."

Richard Branson

EVERY morning, I wake up to an alarm on my iPhone. It then reminds me of the things I have on my morning routine checklist. Getting out of bed, I exercise, usually a run tracked by the Nike+ App listening to Apple Music. I meditate using a combination of Headspace and Calm, then I journal using

Day One. After a breakfast with the family and a shower, I set out to start my workday. Throughout the day I write content (this book for example), send emails to clients and colleagues, create strategies and presentations, usually on my MacBook Air. I have status meetings and pitch presentations that vary from location to location, using the right device for the right situation. Then at night, I unwind with Netflix, I play with my daughter, spend time with my wife, read a little, and then I plan the following day. It's not necessarily a hero's tale, but one of many people like me.

The true hero in the story, however, is the underlying components that allow this day to happen, seamlessly, consistently, and dynamically. And that hero is Apple. Each of my actions whether meditating, writing, presenting, file sharing, or listening to music were all brought to me through an Apple product, service, subscription, or experience. This is the true essence of being an Experience Brand. Understanding a consumer's life so intimately that your brand can create the products, services and experiences needed to empower their individual lifestyle. Sure, I use other products and brands throughout my day, but Apple is my real-life operating system that brings everything together.

So how has Apple created this position in my life? In essence, they have become in an Experience Brand. An evolving entity in my life that continuously and consistently adds value to my day and my life. Apple has grown from a mere product or device manufacturer and into an experience creator, fully utilizing the benefit and opportunity their devices provide. This shift has not only added value to my life but has added massive value to the Apple brand and business through revenue streams beyond product sales. For example, in my day-in-the-life example above, Apple receives revenue from me in the form of device sales, iCloud subscription fees,

App Store purchase and markup fees and News and Music subscription fees to name a few. Some of these recur monthly, some are one-time purchases, and some are exponential purchases. Each interaction or transaction increases the value that I receive as a customer, which simultaneously increases my value to them as a business. One of the most beautiful things about Apple as an Experience Brand, is that I only have one single relationship with them as a brand. I don't have eight different relationships based on the products or services that I buy like many traditional, siloed organizations, but one, simple relationship. As they have scaled their products, services, subscriptions and experiences, they have continued to keep me, their customer, at the center of the experience— making it easy, seamless, and exciting to do business with them. And, as I mentioned earlier, this has paid off in droves in their market valuation, now sitting over $2 Trillion.

This is the story of truly embracing the Experience Brand mindset.

EXPERIENCE BRAND DEFINITION

An Experience Brand is a company that intentionally creates the experience they want their consumers to have in order to do business with them in a symbiotic value progression across their entire supply chain—from their products, services, subscriptions, to experiences. From unawareness, to research, to consideration, and intent to purchase, to consumption, to service and support, to repurchase and loyalty, Experience Brands are continuously manifesting the entire, connected experience their brand should provide at each touchpoint and each moment of interaction. These interactions and moments are then "remembered" and used to progressively create a singular view of the relationship with each customer—continuously evolving the value the brand provides over the lifetime of the customer relationship.

The experiences these brands create can range from removing pain points or chores the consumer has to go through to purchase a product, like financing or shopping, all the way to celebrating the moments of excitement or cherish, like a purchase or repurchase events. These experiences are meant to make the consumer journey as efficient and seamless as possible, while personalizing key moments to aid in decision making or connection to the moment. And within these optimized moments, Experience Brands are finding new opportunities for revenue creation.

REMOVING CHORES

Let's face it, there are certain aspects of your own consumer journey in certain industries that you absolutely hate—whether going into a store, applying for financing, or other issues. These "chores" become moments of avoidance, defection, or drop-off while doing business with a brand. However, they also become opportunities for disruptors or competitors to create new value. Many of these chores are created by years of legacy or silos coming together to create business process, not necessarily to create a positive consumer experience. Whether it's a legacy technology or database, or business units with varying incentives and objectives, these business-created elements produce chores for the consumer. Experience Brands make it their purpose to find these chores and remove them as quickly as possible to ensure their consumers have the most valuable relationship possible with their brand.

On a micro-level, there are some companies that are taking these chores and building entire businesses around solving them:

Uber: Uber didn't create the taxi industry, but they took the chore of calling one, blindly waiting for it to arrive, and often having a poor riding and paying experience and built a lucrative business around it. Uber transparently connected riders with drivers in a seamless click of a button, giving the power to the consumer with a simple question, "Where to?"

Casper: Casper didn't set out to make a superior, innovative mattress. They set out to solve the chore of buying a mattress—going into a store and laying on a mattress while a sales associate awkwardly stands over you explaining how comfortable you are. Casper changed this behavior by connecting different technologies together (bed in a box, e-commerce, and large item logistics) and put the experience behind a click of a button and a 100-night product trial guarantee.

Warby Parker: Warby Parker didn't create eyeglasses, but they made getting stylish, high-quality eyeglasses accessible. In the face of a near monopolistic industry, Warby Parker did a few things to solve consumer pain points. They changed the pricing structure by reducing the amount of markup and overhead for their products. They changed how consumers tried the products by offering five pairs for in-home trial, only sending back the ones you don't like. They also used technology to take this a step further in offering online vision-screening and augmented-reality product trials.

Tesla: Tesla didn't create the automobile, but they changed its role in the marketplace. Leading with the mindset that the automobile is the single, most expensive computer a consumer can buy, Tesla shifted the behaviors an automobile has. With the vehicle itself being an over-the-air receiver,

Tesla has the ability to update its operating system, features and functions in real time to update the vehicle itself, something that, traditionally, would require an entirely new vehicle purchase. Shifting this behavior has taken five to seven years out of the product development lifecycle of the auto industry and turned it into minutes. This innately connects marketing and the product as the updates create moments of excitement and shareability.

CELEBRATING CHERISH

In the evolution of the Journey Economy, consumers are viewing the experience they receive from the brands they buy as a driving factor for their purchase decisions. In fact, according to Gartner's "Customer Experience Survey," 81 percent of marketers expect to compete mostly (or completely) on the basis of consumer experience. This opens up the aperture of how we should be viewing our consumers and how we should be interacting with them. Once the chores are removed, the next phase of an Experience Brand is celebrating moments of cherish, or immersing the consumer into the brand promise in a way that continuously fulfills the relationship between the brand and consumer.

Many companies are starting to capitalize on this opportunity:

Airbnb: Travel is a massive passion point and Airbnb has gone beyond its core service offering of lodging. It provides its consumers with local experiences and journeys. These are provided throughout the shopping process and beyond purchase, giving a holistic experience that goes beyond the product.

Glossier: Glossier has built its brand off the back of a highly successful blog, providing products and experiences for their fanatical readers. The core of its brand is really built around a skincare routine, but each element of the experience from learning about your personal routine, to shopping, to unboxing, to insider physical events, creates moments of joy for their customers. Glossier continues to grow its base by fulfilling its brand promise with each touchpoint, listening to, and connecting its brand to the needs of its customers.

Southwest Airlines: Air travel used to be a luxury. However, Southwest Airlines, over the years has democratized air travel through its low fares created by operational efficiencies, which don't necessarily equate to a poor consumer experience. The experience offerings of no-fee changes, no baggage fees, and the quirkiness of the in-flight staff, have given consumers the ability to feel cherished when engaging with the brand, on their terms. This experience is why it repeatedly ranks highest in customer satisfaction as well as employee satisfaction. The symbiotic relationship between brand and consumer is reciprocated throughout the entire consumer journey.

JOURNEY BASED OPPORTUNITIES: VALUE PROPOSITION

As we can see, the journey a customer takes to do business with your brand is riddled with both pain points and moments of cherish even outside of product usage or service consumption. Each interaction is ripe for adding new value to the relationship with the consumer. This increases the ability to charge a premium for your offerings, find new revenue streams, increase efficiency, and increase the lifetime value of each consumer, all good things for brand growth.

As such, your brand's value proposition is a symbiotic exchange between your brand strategy and consumer expectations. It's a give-and-take relationship and should be designed and orchestrated in a way that creates a continuous, progressive, and seamless experience that fulfills your brand promise with each consumer at each moment of interaction. The value exchange for consumers during this accelerated Journey Economy leans into purpose, experience, ease of transaction, supply chain, logistics, and support, all of which creates a stronger bond between the brand and consumer.

This brings us to two very important pieces of succeeding as an Experience Brand: What value are you creating for your consumer? What economic value do you get in return from the consumer? Answering these questions, we have to look at the evolution of brand strategy and the economics of this value progression.

Evolution of Brand Strategy

Brand strategy has transformed more in the last ten years than ever before. The role brands play in business, in consumers' lives, and in the world, has drastically changed for the better. Brands have a responsibility not only to provide immediate value in products or services, but they must also stand for a purpose and provide an experience. As this happens, and thanks to technology, brands have the responsibility to learn about and progress the relationship between the consumer and the brand on an individual level. As we'll see through this progression, brands become something more than a representation of a business, product, or service, they almost become a self-actualized entity that is used to define key elements of a consumer's lifestyle.

Audience Definition

We can't talk about the evolution of brand strategy without talking about the consumer. The key to any brand strategy, especially as an Experience Brand, is to completely understand the audience or consumer your brand is trying to talk to and affect. Not only do you need to know them as a general segment, but also understand how personal and individual characteristics will come into play as the progression of the relationship unfolds. Mass marketing still has a role in the relationship, but as the consumer provides insights and preferences about themselves, it is our responsibility to use that to provide increased and individual value in return. We'll dig into the details of Audience Development in Chapter 5. But first, let's explore the horizons of brand strategy to understand how value is created from a brand perspective.

BRAND STRATEGY HORIZONS

Vision, Visual, Product, Service — horizon i

Purpose, Experience — horizon ii

Interaction, Relationship Planning, Agility — horizon iii

Self Actualization
Brand Actualization
Brand Activation
Brand Declaration
Status Quo
— horizon iv

Horizon One: Vision, Visual, Product, Service

This stage was the common thought of what a brand is—something that represents a business, product, or service. This is the vision of what the product or service stood for;

the visual and verbal elements like logo, colors, typography, tone of voice, etc.; and the efficacy of the product or service upon consumption or purchase. Horizon One of brand strategy connects the consumer need for a product or service with the colors, tone, and promise of a product that solved a need at its basic level.

Horizon Two: Purpose, Experience

Along came technology like the internet and social media and brands have been forced to become something more. This technological evolution has brought transparency and the consumer voice to the central focal point, giving consumers the power in the brand-consumer relationship.

This expanded brand strategy takes it beyond visual and verbal representation of a business, product, or service and into the next horizon of having a purpose and providing an experience for consumers. Due to this transformation, brands now must stand for something in the world, whether environmental impact, social justice, or cultural causes. At the same time, consumer expectations have grown to become something more than a simple transaction with their brands. They now expect that brands will provide experiences (whether physical or digital) to ease their purchase journeys or immerse them into a brand promise. Understanding both of these shifts, brands are forced to become an experience creator that stands for something versus a product or service provider.

Horizon Three: Interaction, Relationship Planning, Agility

The next brand strategy horizon that is starting to emerge as technology and consumer data become continuous and trackable, is the evolution of an individual relationship with the consumer. The power of an Experience Brand is built at the moment of interaction or non-interaction. At these moments, brand promises are being fulfilled or insight is being developed to provide Experience Brands the information to build new business models. However, what Experience Brands understand about the evolution of brand strategy is that planning these interactions and subsequent interactions evolve into a personalized relationship with their consumers. A relationship strategy that increases the lifetime value of the brand-consumer relationship builds the brand more than any communications or advertising activity ever could.

Horizon Four: Self-Actualization

So, what's on the horizon after relationship planning and execution? The evolution of maintaining and progressing individual relationships is becoming self-actualized and truly living the purpose of the brand strategy across all aspects of the business, all relationships, all communications, and all decisions. With this brand strategy, businesses will be built or transformed with the essence in every fiber of the business. This gives the power to truly define and fulfill the brand's full potential. Something that moves out of a competitive environment and into a cooperative and progressive world.

EVOLUTION OF ECONOMIC VALUE

As brand strategy evolves and the role that brands play in the lives of consumers and the world evolves, the value exchange evolves as well. Not only are consumer expectations growing, but their appetite for paying a premium to meet their expectations grows as well. Building on Pine and Gilmore's Economic Progression model in *The Experience Economy*, we can see that as brand strategy evolves, so does the economic value. The more value your consumers perceive from your brand, the greater its ability to command a premium or engage in longer-term relationships, increasing revenue opportunities. This progressive value gives brands the power to create transformative economics. Therefore, becoming an Experience Brand doesn't just benefit the consumer, but also the bottom line of the business. While exploring the evolution of economic value horizons, we will see how the economics of the Experience Brand in the Journey Economy starts to unfold.

EVOLUTION OF ECONOMIC VALUE

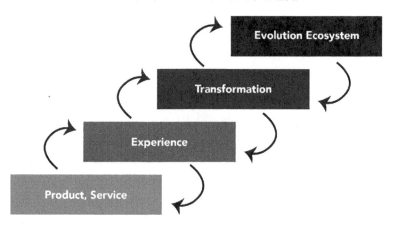

Horizon One: Commodity, Product, Service

The first horizon of economic value is when commodities evolved into products and services. For example, as Pine and Gilmore point out, coffee is a raw commodity, then processed to become a product, then brewed to become a service and finally, as we'll see in the next horizon, it has become an experience thanks to companies like Starbucks, Blue Bottle and others.

However, the thing to understand about this horizon is the growing expectations of consumers. What once was a competitive advantage in the marketplace, quickly takes on the characteristics of a commodity. Meaning that, as competitors emulate market entrants or early adopters, that product, service, or even experience gets commoditized as the cost of entry for a marketplace.

A **commodity** business charges for undifferentiated products.

A **goods** business charges for distinctive, tangible things.

A **service** business charges for the activities you perform.

Horizon Two: Experience

As Pine and Gilmore illustrated in their book, consumer expectations have risen to a point where the experience a brand or company provides around its product or service is becoming almost more important than the product or service itself. This experience, usually seen as a physical, immersive component to a product or service, can now become a digital or digitally connected experience for the consumer. Examples of this are:

Delta's mobile application. Not only does it provide access to the core service of Delta, air travel, but it streamlines the traveler's journey while enabling entertainment and other experiences in the air.

Starbucks has continued to push the boundary on experience. Not only do they provide the epitome of physical experience, but they have enabled a digital component through their rewards program, connecting the digital with the physical by streamlining ordering and checkout, while rewarding customers along the way.

An experience business charges a premium on top of its products and services for the feeling customers get by engaging it.

Horizon Three: Transformation

In their revised version of *The Experience Economy*, Pine and Gilmore expand the idea of experience into what they call "Transformation." This horizon is based on providing a "guest" or "membership" relationship with a brand. These can be delivered through experiences like Disney World or even Wingtip Club, a men's fine clothing brand in San Francisco, where men pay a membership to have access to the store and the experience on top of the cost of the products.

These transformation brands are changing the way that consumers interact with and invite brands into their lives. Not only are they paying for a direct experience with a product or service, but an indirect relationship with the promise the brands are offering, increasing the economic value of the entirety of the brand.

A transformation business charges for the benefit customers (or "guests") receive by spending time there.

Horizon Four: Evolution Ecosystem

Horizon Four is the expansion of how the brand and its products, services, and experiences fit within the lifestyle of their consumers. It is rooted in personalization and preference and provides non-interactions as much as interactions. These business models are built around recurring revenue, which not only provides immediate value to a brand but adds to the long-term prospects and market capitalization.

Professor Scott Galloway uses the term "rundles" to describe this evolution—brands that bundle products and services together under a subscription mindset to deliver recurring revenue. Or 'R(ecurring B)undles.'

This evolution of brand goes far beyond physical and digital experience and into the day-to-day activities of the consumer's life. Examples of this:

Apple, which has moved beyond its core of device manufacturing, and into business models that leverage what the device can do. With innovations into ecosystem connectivity; with device to device integration and cloud storage; to the subscription models of News, Apple TV, Arcade and Music; Apple has been able to package content, service, and product in a way that increases core purchase, but also long-term value in recurring content subscriptions.

Nike has begun moving beyond footwear and apparel. Not only is it continuing to create the culture they want to have, but they have enabled a bundle-based mindset to test new revenue streams. With experiences like Nike Training Club, where members subscribe to get access to online workouts, coaching and training content, and Nike Adventure Club, where parents can purchase subscriptions for their kids allowing them to get new shoes multiple times a year without the hassle of going to a store, trying them on, and purchasing them.

An evolution brand has multiple revenue streams that seamlessly create an entire experience around consumer needs, desires, expectations and lifestyle.

BUSINESS CASE: WINNING IN THE JOURNEY ECONOMY

As we can see, the evolution of brand strategy goes far beyond what we ever imagined brands becoming—even further than what Pine and Gilmore imagined when they first wrote *The Experience Economy* in 1999. The introduction, adoption and expansion of technology has not only empowered consumers to have a stronger role in the brand relationship but has transformed the ability for businesses and brands to create experiences for their consumers, opening the opportunity for differentiated value exchange and revenue.

The brands that are finding growth, the Experience Brands, are using this new dynamic to eliminate the greatest pain points consumers have, elevate those fleeting moments of excitement, and build personalized relationships based on consumer preference, interaction, and consumption. These elements are then intentionally used in a holistic consumer experience that increases the symbiotic value exchange between the brand and each consumer, resulting in reduced cost, increased basket or purchase size, increased premiums, or even net new revenue opportunities. As Apple powers my day-in-the-life, other brands are starting to fill the void in other aspects of my life. The move toward Experience Brands is increasing the short-term economic value of sales as well as the long-term value of the relationship.

As we venture deeper into Experience Brands, we'll not only witness the evolution of consumer expectation and value creation but also the roles that brands will start to play in the lives of their consumers.

 www.JourneyEconomy.com/chapter-3

 #experiencebrand@PaulMiser

LESSONS LEARNED

- An Experience Brand is a brand that intentionally creates the holistic journey it wants its consumers to take in order to do business with it. The Experience Brand strategy creates new value for both the consumer and the brand by removing traditional pain points, expanding moments of joy and creating new interaction opportunities throughout the entire consumer journey.
- Experience Brands operate in a different way from their traditional counterparts. They are extremely consumer focused; they create moments to truly fulfill their brand promise, their operations act as "one unit" to create a singular experience for their consumer; they have the agility to pivot when consumer behaviors change or the marketplace shifts; and they are enabled by technology.
- Experience Brands are evolving the process and outcomes of brand strategy. They move beyond the traditional verbal and visual depiction of a product and service and into how the brand should create and execute interactions. Experience Brand strategy is based on relationship planning and leaning into self-realization as an entity to continually find and create new value.
- Not only do Experience Brands find operational efficiencies by eliminating waste throughout the consumer journey, but the value they create for their customers increases their ability to charge a premium for products and services. Having insight into the consumer and the changing marketplace, they also have the ability to create new business models and revenue streams.

CHAPTER 4

EXPERIENCE BRAND STRATEGY

Putting The Pieces Together

"In preparing for battle I have always found that plans are useless, but planning is indispensable."

Dwight D. Eisenhower

AT THE time when Lincoln Motor Company approached us with a challenge, I had no idea the scale of disruption and transformation many industries were about to face. It was a time in business history where technology hit a point of adoption and efficacy to truly change behaviors and, ultimately, the way business was done. At first glance, Lincoln's challenge seemed simple from an advertising point of view, "We need a new way to grow. Our industry is moving from manufacturing to mobility. Our business model is moving from ownership to membership. We need to prepare our brand and business for this evolution so we can capitalize on these trends." But as we dug deeper in uncovering the truth behind the request, we realized it was not exactly a small task, but something that could determine the fate of, not only an entire company, but could set the stage for an entire industry, an entire movement. If I knew one thing at the time, the answer to this challenge was not going to be as simple as an ad campaign. I knew, that if done correctly, it would require an end-to end-transformation of Lincoln's entire business from vehicle decisions to service offerings to how they made money. In essence, they had to become an Experience Brand. With the challenge set, we embarked on a paradigm-shifting journey.

The journey started with understanding where we were as a brand, and what our value proposition, purpose, and vision were. At the time Lincoln had just gone through an entire brand-strategy refresh, so these refined elements were a great starting point to build from. Their brand and product point of view was all about delivering effortlessness to their customers. This brand strategy took on many forms—from how the products and features were designed, to how the dealer experience was created, all the way through to the advertising and website experience. However, each touchpoint was geared toward communicating this value proposition only from a purchase and ownership perspective—not the entire consumer journey and not to answer the challenge request. Throughout our discovery, we found that this brand strategy provided a solid foundation to translate the necessary elements of an Experience Brand strategy. It gave us a filter to discern insights and opportunities for the customer and the brand experience.

Next, we wanted to intimately understand the issues and

opportunities surrounding the trend elements outlined in their challenge, including manufacturing to mobility, and owner-ship to membership. To establish a broad view of the situation we explored various elements in, around, and adjacent to the brand and industry, as well as more tertiary trends happening in other, non-related industries. We looked at current owner and automotive driver sentiment. We tracked and modeled out customer behaviors as they relate to vehicle ownership and usage. We mapped the end-to-end mobility landscape from direct competitors, upcoming startups, and transportation alternatives. We explored technology trends in, around, and outside of the automotive and mobility industries to see what technologies and behaviors will and should be available to tap into. With this exploration and discovery, we started to get a sense of macro trends that we, as a brand, could authentically start to connect and capture. This exploration gave us both the spatial understanding of what was happening in and around our brand as well as an element of time to ensure we were solving the right challenges at the right moment to ensure product-market fit.

To create the full Experience Brand strategy, we estab-lished a vision and strategic tenets of how the Lincoln brand of effortlessness came to life in the future state of the trends we uncovered in Discovery. This vision provided the blueprint for where the brand needed to go, and the strategic tenets delivered the decision-making criteria to execute in order to reach that vision. Each element was designed to illustrate how the Lincoln brand would capitalize on the appropriate opportunity trends and how the consumer relationship would come to life at key moments, creating the symbiotic value exchange between the brand and the consumer.

Next, we built a series of personas that we could connect the Experience Brand strategy with, offering the right value at the right time. These personas were a spectrum of use cases from ownership to membership, from driving to riding, and everything in between. These use cases gave us the insight and information to build holistic customer experience journeys to find the pain points, moments of joy and opportunities for the Lincoln brand to show up authentically and provide new or increased value to the customers. These customer journeys were built in a progressive manner, showing the transformation from the current state of the brand-consumer relationship and then were modeled out in two-year increments over the course of ten years. These customer journeys captured the gaps from stage to stage in persona growth, technology advancements, mobility trends, and product and service development, to showcase what needs to happen in order to bring the Lincoln Experience-Brand strategy to life.

This progressive consumer journey mapping created the strategic roadmap to define all the things that had to be true in order to execute against the Lincoln Experience-Brand strategy at the right stage. In the end it created a list or backlog of projects that had to be completed at key milestones to move the consumer relationship and the brand forward. By being able to document these projects on a timeline, we could prioritize the projects in a master strategic roadmap to deliver the Experience Brand correctly, over time, learning and optimizing along the way. The outcome of this exercise became the "Lincoln Way," an approach to the experience and lifestyle a consumer receives from being in a relationship with the Lincoln brand. Some of the tactical executions that were derived from this work were:

The Lincoln App: The app that connected the consumer and their preferences to the lifestyle of Lincoln, connecting them to the vehicle by being able to control key features like start/stop, climate control, location, etc; connecting them to their local dealer through service and maintenance updates from the vehicle and the dealer; connecting them to support and lifestyle through on-touch interaction with their personal Concierge.

Mobility Offerings: To lean toward the effortlessness in driving, we partnered with and built mobility offerings that made getting from Point A to Point B more seamless. These offerings included finding parking from the app, location-based gas refueling, and car sharing when traveling.

Service Offerings: We enabled a single point of contact through the Lincoln Concierge that went along with the owners everywhere they went from website to app to dealership, creating a singular relationship with each owner. We built dealer programs that took away pain points from service and maintenance including Pick-up and Delivery for service, where the dealer would come and pick up the vehicle, leave an equivalent or better loaner, and then deliver the vehicle once the service was complete, reducing the pain of going into the dealership.

All of these offerings and more, built a foundation for Lincoln in the mobility and membership space. By taking the consumer experience away from just the financial transaction moments like purchase, service and financing, Lincoln has been able to become more to their members and owners than ever before.

This robust example from Lincoln illustrates the steps needed to define and become an Experience Brand, from research, to strategic development, to customer journeys, into tactical execution of a strategic roadmap. Going through the steps for your brand is crucial to get a deeper sense of what the world looks like in and around your brand and your consumer. This insight gives you massive power to not only define your future and your potential, but also the understanding of what you can do today to move your brand forward. As outlined, Experience Brands are continuously evolving and growing based on consumer behavior and market opportunities, never a moment in the future. And, like the Lincoln example shows above, you can start right where you are by understanding your brand strategy and what it means to your consumers today. With your brand strategy ready, let's break down the steps to define your Experience Brand strategy.

MARKET INTELLIGENCE

As in the Lincoln example, we gained as much intelligence as we could while we were establishing the Experience Brand strategy. Not only did we want to look at information in a moment in time but we also wanted to create the framework and approach to track and reflect over time. By establishing an ongoing market research approach, we were able to understand the trends, behaviors and opportunities that we could leverage to establish the Experience Brand strategy. To best understand the complexity of the opportunities for your brand, you will want to gain intelligence in, around and outside of your industry and your consumer set. With today's connected consumer, behaviors and expectations in a particular industry are affected by 2nd and 3rd level interactions, meaning that the experiences they have in one industry directly affects their expectations of another.

Direct Insight: Looking at your current audience, competitors and industry as well as your organization can give you the information needed to understand the current opportunities for growth. Looking at consumer behavior trends, competitive action and technology trends will allow you to develop the insights needed to optimize your current offerings and find new avenues to create new value within the current environment.

Adjacent Intelligence: The end benefit or value proposition your consumers receive may not be satisfied by your direct industry. They may be getting value from other industries around yours. For example, consumers don't have to own a car to get from one place to another. The rise of ride hailing and car sharing offers an opportunity for consumers to get the end benefit of transportation across different industries. The intelligence you can gather from dissecting your end consumer benefit across other industries will give you more context to consumer behaviors and technology trends giving you the ability to build and create new value propositions for your consumer.

Tertiary Exploration: Tracking and defining more macro trends and consumer behaviors across non-direct industries can give you insight in how consumers are behaving and how technology is affecting their experiences. The experiences consumers are getting elsewhere has a direct effect in what they expect from the experiences they receive from you. If buying a mattress is now as simple as a single click, imagine what that can do to the expectations of renting an apartment or buying a car. This macro view exploration will give you new insight into the trends and behaviors that will ultimately become expectation in your industry.

Ongoing Tracking: The benefit of gaining market intelligence allows you to develop stronger decisions today. However, tracking this intelligence overtime allows you to see emerging trends, consumer expectations, opportunities in the marketplace and understand how value is created for your consumers. This ongoing insight will give you the ability to move beyond the expectations of your current industry and the status quo growth and begin to chart your own course in creating new value over time.

STRATEGIC DEVELOPMENT

The strategic development for an Experience Brand takes your current brand purpose, promise, goals, and objectives and expands them into the elements that truly bring them to life across the consumer journey. Using these elements as input for your Experience Brand strategy, you can begin to see how your brand could and should interact, how it converses with consumers, how relationships should be built over time, establishing trust, expectation, and understanding. This level of experience strategy development gives you the clarity to define, develop, and orchestrate the symbiotic value exchange needed to add massive value to your consumer while finding new revenue and increased efficiencies.

Looking at the pyramid below, you can see that everything your brand does connects the brand purpose with the consumer needs and expectations in these symbiotic value exchanges.

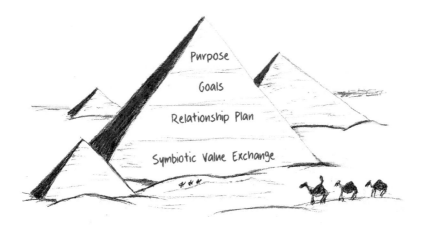

Purpose, Vision, Promise: This is the essence of your brand, what you stand for and what you strive to become.

Goals/Objectives: These are the metrics that you measure your brand against to reach your brand promise while ensuring your business is growing and living up to its full potential.

Interaction/Relationship Planning: Defining the holistic consumer experience, which we'll get to below, you will see how, where, and why your consumers interact with you along their journey to do business with your brand. More and more, these interactions are expected to be connected and progressive from the consumer's perspective. The act of connecting these interactions over time, in a progressive manner, leads you into the planning and development of a relationship.

Symbiotic Value Exchange: The final element in the strategic development is the definition of the symbiotic value exchange between your brand and the consumer. Traditionally, this was at the moment of product consumption or service fulfillment, but in today's Journey Economy, these value exchanges happen all throughout the consumer journey. By understanding, defining, contextualizing, and operationalizing these moments, your brand receives power in the value exchange by overly exceeding your consumers' expectations, while managing the revenue or efficiency opportunities these moments create.

EXPERIENCE BRAND TENETS

With the Experience Brand strategic development established, you and your team will want to define the principles or beliefs your Experience Brand will maintain throughout the development, execution, implementation, and optimization of the strategy and process. These tenets provide crucial consensus and understanding for the organization to aid in process development, decision-making, and identifying moments of pivot or scale. The tenets below are reminders of the Growth Brands we discussed in Chapter 2. Yours will be your own, but these are a great starting point for discussion with your team.

We will put the consumer in the center of our brand strategy.

The foundational tenet for Experience Brands is that they are consumer focused. They are obsessed with making sure they are providing the best possible value to their consumers and building a progressive end-to-end experience for each individual. They completely understand the consumer journey, the pain points and moments of excitement found throughout. They use this journey as a foundation for building their organization from the inside out, allowing each touch point, interaction or non-interaction to solve consumer needs. Being consumer focused, Experience Brands keep an open dialog with their consumers. Whether active or passive, the feedback they receive from their consumers gives them the insight to grow and evolve their organization, operations, and communications, all of which, provides a continuously evolving value proposition for the consumer.

We will not only communicate our brand promise but will fulfill it with each interaction and non-interaction.

While establishing a progressive value proposition to solve for consumer problems or pain points, Experience Brands establish a point of view or purpose in this world, then set out to fulfill this purpose whenever and wherever they can. Many organizations have a brand promise; however, most only try to communicate it. Experience Brands, on the other hand, use the various channels and touch points at their disposal to truly fulfill the promise for the consumer. For example, Uber's brand promise of "Where to?" is fulfilled millions of times each day. Nike's brand promise of "If you have a body, you're an athlete," gets fulfilled with each advertisement, retail experience, app interaction, and even with product usage. And from the Lincoln example above, "effortlessness" was delivered in every decision and execution of their Experience Brand. The integrated network and ecosystem that each brand maintains, provides the ability to fulfill the promise a brand puts forth.

We will connect the holistic consumer experience together to deliver increased value throughout the consumer journey.

Experience Brands look at the entirety of the consumer journey from the consumer's perspective and understand how their brand wants to come to life, then build the operations and supply chain to support it. From customer service, to retail operations, to shipping, to communications, to employee training, to logistics management, Experience Brands look at each interaction across their organization, internal or external, to ensure each is done with the vision of fulfilling their brand promise while maximizing the value exchange with their consumers. Warby Parker has established their entire brand from the inside out, making each interaction, internally or externally, consistent across the entire organization. Netflix has established a Code of Culture that supports the relationships that are built internally, and externally with business partners and, more importantly, with their consumers—all meant to establish a consistent brand and value proposition.

We will establish the systems and frameworks to be agile in the marketplace.

In today's Journey Economy, there is a competitive advantage for the companies that move quickly to market and have the ability to pivot if needed. This doesn't necessarily mean that a company has to be first to market, but it must have the ability to move quickly and react to business and consumer changes. Experience Brands are built around the notion and idea of speed. They believe the faster they can identify consumer problems and pain points, then create solutions to fix them, the faster they can create new value, access new revenue opportunities, and establish a deeper relationship with their consumers. Being consumer focused gives Experience Brands the ability to track the end-to-end journey of consumers and keep an open dialog with them, while identifying the bottlenecks and challenges to solve for. This continuous cycle gives Experience Brands the ability to access the fast-to-market advantage, while maintaining strong relationships with their consumers.

We will use technology to bring our strategy to life, enabling relationships with consumers and improved experiences for our customers.

As some business consultants and venture capitalists would have you believe, not every company is a tech company. However, every Experience Brand is enabled by technology. The rise of the consumer adoption of technology with the increased development of business and data technology, companies gives a unique opportunity to deliver connected, end-to-end experiences that progress individual consumer relationships. Experience Brands use this opportunity to maximize their value propositions, while empowering their brand to fulfill its promise across all touch points, devices, screens, and aisles. They use technology and data to create continuous feedback loops between their consumers and the business throughout their entire journey. This level of intelligence gives Experience Brands the necessary information to make quick decisions to optimize their experiences, pivot if needed, or find new opportunities in the marketplace to capture.

HOLISTIC CONSUMER JOURNEY

So far, we've talked a lot about the consumer journey. Chances are, somewhere in your organization there is a consumer journey established that was done a couple years ago but has yet to be acted on from a holistic perspective. The challenge with large, complex organizations is that there isn't a single steward for the holistic consumer experience, so the consumer journey work that was commissioned by one department falls on deaf ears in other departments. And, in actuality, if the consumer journey was acted upon, it was primarily used to make the marketing process more effective, completely missing out on crucial opportunities in other areas of the journey. Experience Brands, on the other hand, have executive leadership driving the holistic consumer experience strategy and ensuring that it is connected, seamless, and continuously evolving. This is the first step in a successful transformation toward becoming an Experience Brand—having an owner and steward on the executive team that believes in, uses, and evolves a holistic consumer experience strategy. The following aspects are the actions needed to map, develop, and strategize around the consumer journey, once executive leadership has been established.

Consumer Journey Map

Mapping the consumer journey gives a company the insight of what is currently happening as consumers are shopping for, buying from, and getting serviced by companies in your industry. As we've started to explore, this intelligence is highly valuable for corporate development and consumer value creation. The consumer journey map is just that, mapping how consumers currently find out about, research, shop for, buy, consume, and repurchase products and services. An effective consumer journey map showcases the current channels used at specific times, the experience they're currently having, the sentiment at specific moments, how competitors are responding, and when and why they might be abandoning the journey or continuing on. This journey opens up a wealth of knowledge from pain points, to moments of cherish, to bottlenecks, to organizational challenges, all of which become the elements for consideration for the Experience Brand strategy and a strategic roadmap for implementation.

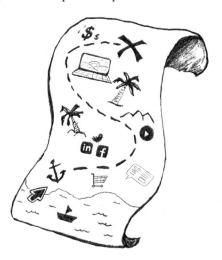

Jobs to be Done

Each interaction point in the consumer journey that is identified is rooted in the idea of consumer "jobs to be done." These are very specific tasks the consumer is trying to solve whether vetting a purchase decision or operating a product. These jobs to be done are the opportunities for brands to help consumers perform the actions faster, more effectively, and more enjoyably. By understanding and owning these Jobs to be Done, brands can intentionally build the experience around the job to fulfill the goals and objectives throughout the consumer journey. These jobs to be done usually come with areas to bring your Experience Brand strategy to life through removing pain points or optimizing moments of joy.

Pain Points and Why

The pain points found in the consumer journey become opportunities for your brand and organization to become operationally efficient while providing incremental value to your customer. These are the moments where consumers feel as though it's a chore or an annoyance to continue in the journey to do business with your brand. This can include going into a store, filling out paperwork, getting financing—really anything that consumers truly don't care for. These pain points are usually created by the additive nature of business over the last 20 years. Meaning, new departments (like service, ownership, digital, e-commerce, brick and mortar) coming online with their own incentive and measurement structure. Instead of integrating these departments into the organization with a consumer-centric lens, they have been created to best serve the business operations.

Removing these pain points not only offers a better consumer experience, increasing the value of the organization and brand, but in some cases, it makes the organization more efficient, reducing costs.

Casper: Casper didn't change the mattress industry. They didn't create a better product. They didn't even invent a new technology. They used the consumer behavior trends of shopping online with the technology called "bed in a box" where mattresses can be rolled into a box for easier shipping. Then Casper set out to solve the biggest pain point in the industry—shopping for a mattress in a store. They knew this awkward encounter of trying a bed in a store with a sales associate standing over you was something that consumers would pay to avoid. And by solving this pain point, they have shifted the overall behaviors of consumer shopping in the mattress category and have started to take market share from some of the more traditional brands.

Uber: Uber didn't change the livery business. They don't have better cars or even faster routes. In fact, they don't even have cars. But they solved the biggest pain point in the livery business—physically hailing or scheduling a car to go from Point A to Point B. Simply by connecting the rider with a driver through an app, Uber has been able to completely transform personal transportation with simplicity, transparency and technology.

Moments of Cherish and Why

On the flipside, doing business with or building relationships with brands we love have moments of excitement for consumers. There are psychological reasons why capitalism works, and as consumers become more conscious with their spending, the relationships built between brand and consumer become opportunities to celebrate moments of cherish. These moments can be receiving a product, fulfilling a service, participating in a cause, or going through an experience.

Disney: Disney has been a master experience provider. From its movie storytelling, to its theme parks and cruises, to its recently introduced Disney+, Disney has established its brand as an experience brand long before the trend was created. The most advanced example of this is their innovation of Disney MagicBands; wristbands guests wear at the Disney theme parks that unlock certain services and offerings. The magic in the MagicBands is consumer data. Each band is loaded with the wearer's personal profile and preference information. Then technology like RFID takes the lead for their personalized and unanticipated experience. The data unlocks line preference, personalized interactions with staff and characters, and even customized experiences throughout the park and their stay.

Tesla: Tesla understands the idea of creating joy and celebrating cherish. From its new product announcements to pre-order programs, everything about the consumer experience is meant to take seemingly normal interactions and turn them into moments of excitement. None is more exciting than the product updates for owners. Tesla has turned the idea of a car into a mindset of "vehicle as hardware." This gives Tesla the ability to provide product updates through software releases versus buying a new vehicle every two years. When these updates hit for owners, the joy, excitement, and moments of cherish are on full display across social media, in communities and across the internet. However, these aren't happenstance. These are intentionally created moments for continued engagement with owners; pushing for lifetime loyalty and easy advocacy.

EXPERIENCE BLUEPRINT AND STRATEGIC ROADMAP

As in the Lincoln example above, we mapped the consumer journeys against different timeframes in the future not only to understand how the Experience Brand strategy unfolds over time, but also to give us the information needed on which activities and projects the company had to take on today to get to the next stage in the Experience Brand strategy. These progressive consumer journeys do a couple of things. First, they are used to create the Experience Blueprint. This is a detailed tactical view on how the designed consumer experience comes to life for the consumer across the organization whether people, process, or technology. The Experience Blueprints become the playbook for specific touchpoints and interactions we're trying to eliminate, optimize or expand as a part of our Experience Brand strategy. We'll drill into the details of this in the next chapter.

Second, it defines the gaps between the time-based journey maps of the Experience Brand strategy across people, process and technology from stage to stage. These gaps become the elements of the Strategic Roadmap. To execute an experience in the consumer journey, certain organizational elements have to be orchestrated to give the consumer what you're expecting to provide. Each of these initiatives are prioritized to make the biggest immediate impact for your value proposition with your brand experience. This strategic roadmap, which could last over the course of five or ten years, gives your organization a collective view of what to accomplish and why. One thing to understand about evolving into an Experience Brand is that it is a continuous approach to becoming a more valuable brand for your consumers.

This approach also gives your organization the ability to react more quickly in the marketplace as things change based on insight from the consumer, competitors, behaviors or technology. Having this agility is a driving force from the continued and exponential growth of Experience Brands. Executing in the Continuous Beta mindset, Experience Brands are continuously maximizing their consumer journeys. During Part 4, we'll talk through the details of the organizational operations that Experience Brands implement for this level of success.

A great example of a company who has embraced the Experience Blueprint and Strategic Roadmap is Delta Airlines. Over the last ten years it has been executing its Experience Brand strategy by continuously eliminating pain points and maximizing moments of joy its customers. It has established its Experience Blueprint and Strategic Roadmaps in staged experiences based on consumer behavior, technological advances, competitive advantages and the like. Each stage starts with an end-to-end consumer journey with the specific touchpoints they want to enable and when. Then that is broken down into tactical projects. For example, when creating their first iteration of their mobile app, they defined their strategy for the mobile app tracking rewards and loyalty, which they expected would give them the adoption and traction to gain new insight from their customers. The next consumer journey stage used the app to streamline the check-in process which enabled new experiences beyond that. As their consumer journey stages evolved, Delta has established innovations like their app, in-flight entertainment, check-in procedures, Sky Club, and Sky Miles, making their brand irreplaceable for their consumer base. As they evolve into the future, they are looking beyond devices and into biometrics and RFID to expedite the process and optimized their experience even further.

Establishing a corporate-wide Experience Brand strategy sets the vision and the path toward becoming an Experience Brand. The strategic roadmap is the tool used to implement that vision, something that is a continuous approach and always evolving into the future.

Pilots / Test / Scale

Once established, the initiatives on the Strategy Roadmap become projects that can be put into market quickly. Leveraging the Lean Startup methodology, popularized by Eric Reis, Experience Brands use the idea of the iteration of MVPs (minimum viable products) to get to market quickly, to gather consumer feedback, to learn, iterate and grow. The success of Experience Brands comes from their ability to do this quicker and more strategically than their competitive set and industry. By establishing this process and methodology, Experience Brands can continue to progress toward their strategies by operating on a rapid decision-making process that is built into the approach. The decisions to keep, optimize, scale, pivot, or kill a solution is determined on the feedback and results it gets in the marketplace. By keeping and evolving the strategic roadmap of initiatives to tackle, Experience Brands are continuously iterating, making the consumer experience stronger and more valuable for each and every consumer with whom they interact.

Another great example of this is Amazon Prime. It wasn't always the membership operating system across the Amazon ecosystem that it is now, offering discounts, expedited shipping, access to content and services for a monthly fee. It started simply as a subscription for free two-day delivery. It has become a behemoth in the marketplace, not because they launched it in its current state, but because they launched it, learned from it, iterated on it, and grew the value over the last 15 years.

Now let's get to work and do the same for your brand.

RAMPING UP YOUR EXPERIENCE BRAND

Transforming into an Experience Brand doesn't have to be a departure from the direction you are currently heading. In fact, it's advisable to start with where you are today to determine where you need to go tomorrow and into the future. With Lincoln, we didn't set out to stop selling cars. Rather, we were building the strategy for the day where car sales weren't the only source of revenue and value with consumers. We deliberately started with the value proposition of today to identify how we could maximize the value of that value proposition for our current customers—while intentionally setting the stage for the future behaviors we want to change. For example, the implementation of the mobile app first was an intentional move to shift the customer's relationship with the brand from a turn of a key to a tap of a button. That one behavioral change opens up worlds of future opportunity. Delta understood this as well when they embarked on their decades-long journey toward becoming an Experience Brand.

The Experience Brand strategic approach detailed in this chapter gives us the recipe for value creation from your customer's perspective. By starting with the trends and behaviors surrounding your brand, products and services as they stand today, you gain tremendous insight into the expectations and opportunities waiting to unfold. Connecting these insights to a series of consumer journey maps, you can develop your Experience Brand strategy to continuously and progressively create value for your consumer. The gaps between your staged consumer journey maps become your Experience Blueprint and Strategic Roadmap that gives you clarity in how to act and what to do to deliver that action.

As we get into the execution framework in the next chapter, you'll uncover the tactics needed to fulfill you Experience Brand strategy.

 www.JourneyEconomy.com/chapter-4

 #experiencebrandstrategy@PaulMiser

LESSONS LEARNED

- The best place to start to evolve your brand into an Experience Brand is where you are today. By exploring your current brand strategy and how it can authentically remove pain points and celebrate moments of joy in your current consumer journey, you can begin to create more value for your consumer and your brand. Start today and plan for the future.

- When finding and defining the opportunities for new value creation for your Experience Brand, you have to look on the different levels of focus. Start closely with your organization, direct competitors, and your industry. Then, work outwards to indirect and adjacent companies and industries. Finally, look at the non-direct or tertiary companies and trends. This holistic point of view will give you the insight needed to identify the consumer behaviors, technologies and organizational trends that will allow you to find new opportunities to authentically bring your Experience Strategy to life.

- The Strategic Development framework of an Experience Brand is similar to many strategic planning initiatives. Including vision, goals, objectives, and tactics, the Experience Brand strategy solves for different metrics and KPIs—ones focused on consumer experience and value, measured against both the short-term and long-term.

- The most valuable thing a company has at its disposal is a Consumer Journey Map. By capturing and tracking the consumer's journey to do business with your brand, you get a wealth of information surrounding device, jobs to be done, sentiment, competitive actions, pain points, moments of joy, etc. These data points will be used to transform your brand into an Experience Brand by leveraging them to create a consumer-centric relationship that continuously creates value for the consumer.

- By creating and understanding the priorities in the consumer journey map, strategic development of your Experience Brand can truly begin. By having clarity on value and consumer expectations, your Experience Brand strategy can establish the framework of vision, mission, goals and objectives from an enterprise brand perspective to best leverage the entirety of the consumer experience for business success.

CHAPTER 5

EXPERIENCE BRAND FRAMEWORK

BECOMING AN EXPERIENCE BRAND

"We see our customers as invited guests to a party, and we are the hosts. It's our job every day to make every important aspect of the customer experience a little bit better."
Jeff Bezos

ONCE we had the Lincoln Experience-Brand strategy defined, we moved quickly into execution. The essence of an Experience Brand is having the ability to move quickly and intelligently in the marketplace, while intentionally developing the consumer experience you want your consumers to have. This leads to a differentiated approach to execution. Instead of a linear project of defining all future requirements then executing until perfect before launch, Experience Brands use a systems-thinking framework to continuously execute their strategy. In Lincoln's case, we had a series of five consumer journeys spanning a ten-year timeframe. Going in, we knew that the tenth year consumer journey was based more on assumption than fact, but we established the Strategic Roadmap to deliver experiences leading to that vision to prove or disprove the assumptions, providing valuable insight for strategy refinement by continuously tracking consumer behavior, industry trends and market opportunities as we put things into market in the earlier staged consumer journeys. This framework gives the brand and the business the collective organizational intelligence to not only understand consumer needs, but also to respond to and even predict the needs in the future.

The best way to start gathering this intelligence and driving your Experience Brand strategy forward is to get your experiences into market as quickly as possible to see how they perform. The process of doing this is detailed throughout all of Part 4 of this book, but the development of the framework is what this chapter is all about. Here, we'll discuss the detailed tactics of your Experience Brand strategy that will build in the elements for continuous learning, iteration, and innovation.

EXPERIENCE BRAND FRAMEWORK

There are three foundational elements for the Experience Brand framework that allows your brand and organization to capitalize on the opportunities found in the Journey Economy, while building the ability to pivot and evolve as consumer or business needs shift. The elements of the framework are meant to ensure your brand is defining, tracking, progressing, and rewarding the relationships with your consumers while gaining the organization intelligence to capitalize on new opportunities. Having this level of understanding gives your brand the ability to gather direct and indirect feedback from consumers, understand new pain points within the consumer journey, and develop a level of continuous intelligence, making your value propositions stronger—all while becoming more collaborative and efficient as an organization, reducing costs while finding new avenues for revenue.

The core elements of the framework are:

- Audience Development

- Experience Orchestration

- Experience Brand Technology Stack

These framework elements become the foundational thread for the Growth Action Plan detailed in Part 3, giving you the ability to intentionally create growth that fulfills your brand's potential in the marketplace.

AUDIENCE DEVELOPMENT

The most crucial element of any Experience Brand is the consumer. Fully defining and understanding the consumer at the outset of your Experience Brand implementation gives you a strategic starting place to appropriately execute your experiences for growth. Having established segments and personas gives you the ability to both track key behaviors to learn from while monitoring for other segments and personas that may be beneficial to the brand. This intelligence will allow your brand to not only optimize and maximize your current Experience Brand strategy, but also find new market opportunities to capture. Getting the details of the audience right at the beginning of your implementation will only make your Experience Brand strategy and brand growth stronger and more effective. This section outlines how to define and build effective audience segments and personas. These personas will be used as models around which to orchestrate the moments of your Experience Brand.

Consumer Behaviors and Audience Definition

By establishing the audience framework, we will be able to develop the appropriate value propositions, demand creation and capture strategies; map out the right consumer journeys; and then create the progressive triggers that capture inputs that build into value-added relationships. This framework starts at a high level of audience segmentation, becomes more defined as personas, and then establishes the mechanisms to build personalized relationships with real consumers as they interact with and consume brands. The journey from audience segment to personalization is rooted in trust, value, and data. Especially in today's highly tumultuous consumer privacy environment, the way Experience Brands establish this trust by capturing, using, and recapturing data is, in itself, a showcase of value between brand and consumer. Experience Brands understand the value of long-term relationships and only capture and use data in a way that is considerate to their consumer and adds value to the relationship.

Audience Segmentation

We should all be extremely aware of who we're trying to affect with our products, services, experiences, and brands. However, this is only the starting point. Understanding the segments of the population that will find the most value in what we are building or creating gives us a starting point to develop personas. Segmentation is building homogeneous subgroups of people based on demographics, geographics, psychographics, and product usage, along with media and communication behaviors to establish a high-level view of the consumer to whom we are talking. It is a general view of where we can connect age, psychographics and geography together to generate a basic understanding of the people we are trying to target and their expectations.

Examples of audience segments are:

- Millennial Dads in Chicago suburbs
- Boomer Empty-Nesters in Cleveland
- Young Professionals from Ivy League schools in Boston
- Chief Engineers at Aerospace companies
- Marketing Managers at Financial Services companies in San Francisco

Within each segment there will be even more nuance to individuals that can be further explored and defined. This is where the persona comes into play.

Personas

Personas are detailed human representations of subgroups of segments. Personas are usually established as fictional characters that represent these subgroups built to best understand the nuance of the individuals we are servicing with our brand, products, service, and experience. Personas are built as descriptive manifestos that define the psychology, goals, fears, personality types, likes or dislikes, expectations, and "days in the life" of the specific individual our brands are trying to affect.

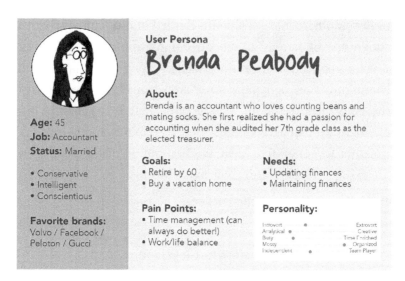

User Persona

Brenda Peabody

About:
Brenda is an accountant who loves counting beans and mating socks. She first realized she had a passion for accounting when she audited her 7th grade class as the elected treasurer.

Age: 45
Job: Accountant
Status: Married

- Conservative
- Intelligent
- Conscientious

Favorite brands:
Volvo / Facebook / Peloton / Gucci

Goals:
- Retire by 60
- Buy a vacation home

Pain Points:
- Time management (can always do better!)
- Work/life balance

Needs:
- Updating finances
- Maintaining finances

Personality:

Introvert	●	Extrovert
Analytical ●		Creative
Busy	●	Time Enriched
Messy		● Organized
Independent	●	Team Player

The persona becomes the starting point to data capture for true personalization and relationship planning. This data capture will be based on preference, usage, interaction, sentiment, and product or service consumption.

Tiered Consumer Relationships

In today's business environment there are many forms that consumer relationships can take. There are traditional business-to-business (B2B) relationships, where businesses market to other businesses. There are business-to-consumer (B2C) or direct-to-consumer (DTC) relationships, where brands and businesses create direct relationships with their consumers. And there are business-to-business-to-consumer (B2B2C) relationships, where the consumer builds a relationship with both a product brand and the intermediary brand. A great example of this is in the automotive industry, where the consumer ultimately has to develop a relationship with a local dealer as well as a relationship with the auto brand itself.

Understanding the nuance and dynamics of your particular

situation will give you insight into how the relationships could and should be built for your brand and in your industry. In the direct relationships of B2B and B2C, your brand has a lot of control in what happens in the consumer journey and how you can structure direct relationships with the consumers. However, in the tiered B2B2C relationships, there will always be the challenge of who really owns the relationship with the consumer, and, in turn, who owns the consumer data. The ultimate challenge here is the ability to continue to find value for the consumer, while removing pain points in their journey.

EXPERIENCE ORCHESTRATION

With the details of the personas and the varying types of consumer relationships defined, now is the time to orchestrate the experiences you've defined in your consumer journey maps and experience blueprints. The components of the experience blueprints are those specific use cases or micro user journeys that are built to remove pain points or optimize moments of joy. Experience Orchestration is the detailed process that delivers the experience that you want to build for your consumer. Activating all available assets at your disposal from a consumer perspective and an organizational perspective, your experience will come to life using data, technology, platforms, people, and content.

For example, when we were building the mobile app for the Lincoln Experience Brand strategy, one use case that we built against was remotely starting your vehicle. From a consumer perspective, we wanted to add as much effortless value into that task as possible, seamlessly and simply. When users opened their app, we delivered a personalized welcome message based on the time of day, a large start stop button, door lock and unlock buttons, access to climate control and depending on the weather, traffic, and the driver's calendar integration, we offered up the ability to start a route to their next appointment. We defined that moment in time for the driver, then used many different data sources, integrations and consumer elements to bring that moment in time to life, repeatedly, consistently and at scale. This is one example of many Experience Orchestrations in the Lincoln consumer journey.

Experience Brands orchestrate their experiences through the practice of service design and process maps to ensure the right things happen at the right time for the consumer and the organization.

Service Design & Process Maps

Service Design is the practice of coordinating and aligning the different elements needed to bring an experience to life. Whether people, process, content, data, technology or platform, each element is given a role and response based on specific triggers in the consumer experience journey. These service designs can range from simple use cases like a consumer calling into a customer support line and associating the phone number with the user profile to start that call off personalized and informed all the way to more complex use cases like that of the Lincoln example above where multiple data points, integrations and vehicle connectivity are leveraged to bring the experience to life. Effective service design for Experience Brands are both continuous and progressive, outlining what happens during the experience, what happens after and how that experience interaction is stored for the next experience a consumer takes with your brand strategy.

EVIDENCE	Website	Retail Location	Employees/ Purchasing	Purchase
CUSTOMER JOURNEY	Visit website	Visit store, browses	Discuss features, prices	Transaction activity
FRONTSTAGE		Welcomes to store	Gives purchase information	
	Support chat			Automated calls
BACKSTAGE ACTIONS	Responds to chat questions	Inventory	Fulfillment queue	Accounting
SUPPORT PROCESSES	Analytics logs visitor	Foot traffic scanner	Payment process	Distribution/ Delivery

This approach of systematic service design not only gives you the blueprint to build against, but it creates the foundation and data to learn from the experiences for future iterations of the experience or consumer challenge you're trying to solve. Executing the Service Design takes the form of process maps and build requirements for each of the elements needed to support the ideal experience. These process maps are categorized in two broad categories: Front End, meaning what happens from a consumer perspective; and Back End meaning what happens behind the scenes to bring the experience to life.

Front-End: The front-end of an orchestrated experience is what the consumer ultimately experiences. These are the mobile apps, the websites, the in-store interactions or customer support actions that give the consumer the experience you want to manifest. The front-end of the orchestration is what the consumer will remember and will become the expectation for them as they progress through the relationship with your brand.

Back-End: The back-end of an orchestrated experience is the hard-working elements of your organization and brand that enables the front-end experience. These elements are the data, technology platforms, content, people and transactions that are used to orchestrate the front-end experience for the consumer. The push-pull environment of the back-end is used to create the experience while capturing new data and insight to deliver subsequent and progressive experiences.

The technology requirements defined and built into the service design and process maps are then translated into an Experience Brand Technology Stack.

Experience Brand Technology Stack

A driving force for the development of an Experience Brand is technology. Enabling the right technology and data strategy not only powers the Experience Brand strategy, but it also opens up new value and revenue opportunities along the way. By harnessing the power of technology and data, Experience Brands can capitalize on interactions and create value-added non-interactions. They can develop, measure, and track their consumers to develop true, one-to-one relationships based on the preferences and data they provide. This information moves Experience Brand value beyond product or service and into experience and relationship development, expanding short-term and lifetime value for each consumer. Technology isn't just something that enables marketing, but it connects experiences, expands on what is possible for product development, creates personalized experiences and offerings for consumers, and makes both the consumer's and your employees' lives more seamless and efficient.

Platforms

As consumers and employees become more and more connected to devices, the role of digital platforms and tools expand in value throughout the consumer journey. Whether it's a website, app, kiosk, or voice-enabled device, platforms give consumers and employees new ways to interact with each other and the brand. Using platforms to capture and deploy data can create enriched and personalized interactions and even have the power to completely remove interactions that were once deemed painful for the consumer. As we reach peak screen time, non-interaction platforms will become increasingly important for Experience Brands moving forward.

Customer Profiles

Building on consumer data and the platform and physical interactions, unified profiles can and should be developed. These profiles allow a brand to get a singular view of the consumers with whom they are interacting in order to best serve and fulfill the brand promise for the individual consumer. These consumer profiles can be aggregated, accessed, and reconciled with each interaction across channels, whether digital, physical, or social, connecting first, second, and third level data. Moving forward, as privacy continues to play a bigger role, the more a brand can capture first party data, the more intimate and detailed the relationship between brand and consumer can become.

Data

Data plays a big role in any aspect of business these days; especially for Experience Brands. Not only do they use it to target and track their consumers for advertising effectiveness, but they use it to completely transform their business and the value for their consumer from the inside out.

Data, in the business world, has an extremely complex perception. On one hand, people view data as a savior for all things business. On the other, it has become a cause for paralysis by either having too much, not enough, or it isn't actionable. With all its hype and all its let downs, data, when used correctly, can become a key driver to business. And as we're witnessing from Experience Brands, data can be that connective tissue within the organization, within the ecosystem, and within each relationship with the consumer. Data plays many roles for Experience Brands, so differentiating these roles will give you the insight as to what to look for, what to track, how to communicate, and how to implement in your Experience Brand journey.

The evolution of data usage should help a company become more operationally efficient, become more effective in marketing and communications, and ultimately create better products, services, and experiences for consumers.

Analytics and Bottlenecks

Experience Brands know what to measure, how to measure it, and what insights need to be derived in order to form the best view of their organization. Creating this level of transparency and insight, Experience Brand leaders use analytic data to get a holistic view of their organization in both the past and present, then create the appropriate models to identify trends for the future. This view not only provides the right intelligence to make smarter and more thorough business decisions, but it also provides insight into bottlenecks in the organization, pain points for consumers, and moments of excitement or opportunity for value creation. Experience

Brands use analytic data to build the foundation for their data strategy.

Operational Efficiency

The next evolution of data is to use it to become operationally effective. The root of most disruption in the marketplace has been by new insurgents or reinvented incumbents becoming more operationally effective around complex business operations or consumer pain points. Operational efficiency not only increases profit margins for the business, but it also enhances the consumer's experience for the brand, product, or service, making it easier to do business with your organization.

Marketing Effectiveness

Next in the evolution of the Experience Brand data strategy is using data to best segment, target and market a brand, product, service, or experience. By becoming functionally effective in the marketing capacity of an organization, Experience Brands have the ability to connect a value proposition and re-establish operational efficiency with the correctly segmented audiences. This aids in more efficient demand creation and more effective capture—establishing an always-on marketing engine between brand and consumer to continuously connect on a personal level with each individual customer.

Journey Connection and Continuation

As marketing has evolved and the experience has become a driving force for consumer decision making, the concept and strategy of the consumer journey has become a competitive advantage for Experience Brands. The landscape in which brands have to create, market, communicate, and sell products and services has drastically changed from a handful of channels and mediums into a splintered, yet diversely personalized environment where no one strategy will work for everyone and every brand. Brands now have to reach consumers across screen, device, and aisle, and they are being forced to ensure that as consumers make these transformations across channels, the relationship and experience is consistent and progressive. This is where Experience Brands leverage consumer interaction and preference data to connect the journey from touchpoint to touchpoint to move the relationship forward, continuously adding value to the consumer along the way.

Personalization & Relationship Planning

Personalization has largely been considered as the pinnacle of big data and marketing. However, Experience Brands view personalization more as a value-driven opportunity than a pure marketing play. Personalization and relationship planning go far beyond marketing, advertising, and communications and into product and service development and experience creation, increasing the individualized product-market fit and development. Sure, personalization helps in the marketing realm, but Experience Brands are continuously looking at the holistic consumer experience to identify areas of insight to remove pain points, maximize cherish, or find new opportunities for value and revenue creation.

Experiential

The final step in an Experience Brand data strategy evolution is the use of personalization to create experiences at certain relationship, membership, or brand-established triggers. This experiential evolution gives brands the ability to differentiate in the marketplace. As consumer expectations evolve and experiences become commoditized as table stakes for competition, these experiential moments become opportunities to continue to expand upon the relationships and provide new value propositions.

ESTABLISHING THE PRACTICE

Transforming your organization to become an Experience Brand is a combination of brand strategy and technology all put to work through orchestrated experiences of service design created by consumer journeys. By fully understanding your audience segments and personas you can design the experiences needed to capitalize on key areas in your consumer journey. This orchestration coming to life on the front-end for the consumer is a carefully constructed process map on the back-end of your organization, pulling together data, technology, people, content and transaction in the appropriate way.

Bringing these orchestrated experiences to life for your Experience Brand consistently, repeatedly and progressively, you will need to build detailed personas, create the service designs and process maps and establish a robust technology and data stack that delivers the instantaneous response for the consumer action. This combination of front-end and back-end gives you the ability to better capture information on your consumer while providing them the next best action to take to progress the relationship. As these orchestrated experiences come to life, the progressive nature of the consumer-brand relationship will create the end-to-end consumer journey for your Experience Brand. Building and leveraging your technology stack appropriately allows these experiences to be as automated as possible while giving you the analytics and intelligence to continuously optimize your experiences while finding new opportunities to capture.

Having the foundation set, we can now put your Experience Brand to work using the Growth Action Plan.

www.JourneyEconomy.com/chapter-5

#experiencebrandframework@PaulMiser

LESSONS LEARNED

- Fully understanding, defining and creating audience segments and personas will build the foundation for the Experience Brand strategy. Not only will these be used to develop the strategy but will also be used to establish the basics for data targeting, capture, tracking, and usage.

- Knowing the moments and experiences you want to create for your customers, you can establish a service design practice that details the elements needed to bring those experiences to life. Leveraging all assets available to you, you can plot out the actions and reactions that must happen consistently to give your consumer the experience you want them to have.

- Executing the service designs and process maps requires elements on the front-end that are enabled by the actual consumer interaction as well as the back-end, which are the organizational elements used to orchestrate the front-end. By activating data, technology, people, content and transactions, the orchestration of your brand becomes an organization-wide activity, while simultaneously maximizing the experience for your customer.

- The Experience Brand technology stack is developed and activated to systematically and repeatedly bring your experiences to life. It becomes a create-and-capture machine enabling the orchestrated experiences while capturing interaction and consumer data to move the relationship forward to the next action.
- Data becomes the lifeblood and linchpin for the activities of your Experience Brand strategy. Using the audience as the foundation, you can create detailed definitions of your segments to best target them, capture data from them, and use that data to respond to an interaction. This data provides increased analytics to measure, optimize, or pivot on the strategy.

PART 3

EXECUTION

The Growth Action Plan

"You don't have to be great to start, but you have to start to be great."

Zig Ziglar

CHAPTER 6

GROWTH ACTION PLAN OVERVIEW

WINNING IN THE JOURNEY ECONOMY

"Quality in a service or product is not what you put into it.
It is what the customer gets out of it."

Peter Drucker

SO FAR, we've seen the definition and development of the detailed strategy and framework to begin your Experience Brand transformational journey. This section is geared to put that strategy to work. The Growth Action Plan is a tactical approach to execute your Experience Brand by systematically and predictably capturing and creating growth through ongoing symbiotic value exchanges with your consumer. This Growth Action Plan gives you the vision and tools to capitalize on the paradigm-shifting Journey Economy through explicit and intentional end-to-end brand transformation.

Executing as an Experience Brand requires a whole-of-company approach to ensure the organization is providing increasing and progressive value to the consumer across the entirety of their journey. Experience Brands, that continue to find success, implement an ongoing growth action plan that evolves as the relationship with the consumer grows and as the company matures in its value propositions. This approach produces both short-term results for the organization and brand as it builds toward long-term success in lifetime value, operational efficiency, incremental revenue, and net-new revenue opportunities. This Growth Action Plan starts with the basics of building strong consumer relationships from the very first interaction and is continuously iterated, optimized, and evolved across the organization as the relationship grows deeper.

THE GROWTH ACTION PLAN

The Growth Action Plan is made up of four distinct actions; however, none are mutually exclusive. All are connected to execute the Experience Brand strategy in a functional way. The progressive nature of being an Experience Brand provides insight into the audience, their expectations, their consumer journey, and the value opportunities in a real-time basis, giving you the ability to not only progress from action to action, but to continuously optimize and iterate each action as a standalone, adding more and more value over time. Starting with the basics of Experience Brand marketing, traveling through the new world of commerce and harnessing the power of membership over ownership, this Growth Action Plan allows you and your brand to create new ways of growth with your current value propositions and find new business models to deliver new value throughout the end-to-end consumer journey.

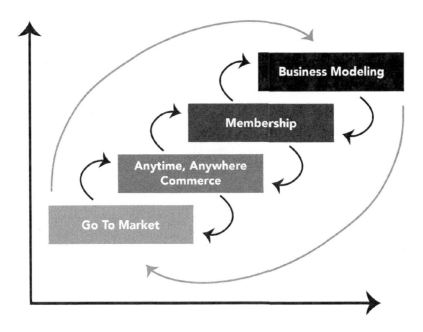

Action 1: Go to Market

Reinventing the demand-creation and customer-acquisition process requires more in the Journey Economy. Not only do brand messaging and performance marketing need to work in concert, but marketing must be integrated across the consumer journey with product, commerce, transaction, service, and support. This integration shifts the focus from demand creation to demand capture putting emphasis on the organic nurturing of consumer transactions and growth—to be scaled through paid media. Experience Brands lead with the mindset of "retention first," providing an experience or lifestyle that their consumers want to be a part of, not just buy from. With this mindset as the foundation, Experience Brands operate as a "machine," not just creating demand but capturing it in a way that adds value to the consumer-brand relationship even prior to a formal, purchase transaction.

Action 2: Anytime, Anywhere Commerce

Retail isn't dead; it's just different. Building on the Consumer Journey Mapping exercise and the Go to Market strategy, Experience Brands quickly find that the actual transaction or purchase becomes a pain point for many industries and consumers. Experience Brands implement an Anytime, Anywhere Commerce strategy to best fulfill the needs and expectations consumers have for transactions on their terms. This strategy includes building an interconnected ecosystem of commerce, matching brick and mortar with e-commerce, social, mobile, or marketplace channels. Then connecting those channels with consumer data and preferences, to create a personalized journey where the transaction happens organically rather than as a separate interaction.

Action 3: Membership

As Experience Brands lead with a retention-first mindset and offer a seamless transaction experience, they must fulfill their brand lifestyle promise at every interaction post-purchase. Creating a Membership strategy that truly fulfills this brand promise gives Experience Brands the ability to continuously engage and interact with their consumers, offering incremental value during the ownership phase of the relationship. This continuous engagement fosters opportunities for loyalty, increased customer support, advocacy, and ultimately repurchase.

Action 4: Business Models

When Experience Brands are operating across the entirety of the consumer experience from Go to Market, to Commerce, to Membership, they have the opportunity to engage with and learn about their consumers in a much more intimate manner. This insight gives Experience Brands the ability to fully understand consumer pain points, missed expectations, and white-space opportunities to deliver exponential value for their consumers. These opportunities manifest in the transformation of business models, where economic value is created by shifting the value that brands fundamentally offer to their consumers. By expanding horizontally or vertically or by bundling and unbundling features, products, services, or experiences, Experience Brands can build new ways to create revenue.

GETTING STARTED

To succeed in the Journey Economy, brands need to be extremely focused on the entirety of their relationship with their consumer. From marketing to sales to ownership to the actual business model, brands have the decision to either create progressive value for their consumer or break the relationship. Starting today with what you know about becoming an Experience Brand, you can make the decision to create new, progressive value for your consumer as well as your brand. Just by executing the following Growth Action Plan, you can break out of the status quo and harness the winds of change in your favor. This is the moment where you can become a seasoned sailor for your brand, your organization and yourself.

www.JourneyEconomy.com/chapter-6

#growth@PaulMiser

CHAPTER 7

GO TO MARKET STRATEGY
LEADING WITH RETENTION FOR ACQUISITION

"The purpose of a business is to get and keep a customer.
Without customers, no amount of engineering wizardry, clever
financing, or operations expertise can keep a company going."
Theodore Levitt

DOES this scenario sound familiar in your organization?

Our sales have declined in the last two years. So, in order
to kickstart sales, our Executive team has decided we need a
new Go to Market strategy that gets a new product or feature
into the marketplace and "creates buzz." The request then

quickly turns into developing an advertising campaign geared to acquire new customers. This will give sales the boost we need to meet our business goals and objectives— after all, it's worked in the past. So, your company hires an ad agency with the brief to create buzz and drive acquisition. You brief the agency to generate the most awareness possible with the right offer driven by mass media—again, all of this has worked in the past. The agency goes away to create the best campaign money can buy. Three to six months later, your big campaign has been approved through your organization and is in market and your media is activated and running. Big things to come, right? Or are they?

Three months later, you haven't seen the sales uptick you were expecting. Not to worry, this happens all the time. You shift your messaging hoping that will do the trick to get new people aware of your new product and features with the right call to action to drive them to purchase. This time, big things really are coming.

Six months later, the media has run its course and the campaign is over. Looking at the entirety of the campaign, you notice it has not come close to hitting benchmarks you set out to hit. And, the sales that you did receive were attributed to incentives that were offered and were one-hit sales that resulted in a loss for the organization with low probability of a repeat purchase or increased lifetime value. It seems the old playbook of advertising has missed the mark and not returned the value on the investment.

So, what happened? To put it simply, the rules of Go to Market strategies have changed. Media has become fragmented and individualistic with information personally curated, and consumers have begun to expect more from brands before they buy. What once was a simple equation of messaging and media has evolved into a playbook of consumer journey mapping, a retention mindset, and action-reaction engagements until a consumer makes a purchase decision. Experience Brands use Go to Market strategies as a simple introduction to the brand, product or service, but once that introduction is created, it's what they do next that makes them successful.

GO TO MARKET OVERVIEW

Transforming the first phase of the Experience Brand strategy is the evolution of Go to Market—creating a new journey for consumers to learn about, engage with, decide on, and ultimately purchase your brand offering. Experience Brands effectively turn this journey into an all-encompassing experience by leading with a retention mindset, creating brand experience strategies, algorithmic actions and dynamic messaging so that consumers can fully experience the brand lifestyle before purchase. Establishing this type of technology-driven, organic marketing strategy, the Experience Brand Go to Market approach delivers content, messaging, interactions, product trials, offers, and purchase actions based on different consumer behavior, interaction, or contextual triggers. This increases opportunities to personalize the entire experience progressively to deliver the right content, the right message, the right context to the right person for a purchase decision and transaction.

Experience Brands leverage this type of Go to Market strategy not only to learn about their consumers in extreme detail, but also to identify the opportunities to create enhanced value for them, with an always-on, active and passive, feedback loop with their consumers. They use this valuable information to craft and curate the best way to continually engage and retain consumers' interest as they interact with the brand.

From advertising and marketing efforts, to website visits, to in-store walk-ins, to sales appointments, Experience Brands not only have a plan for each touchpoint and interaction, but for all subsequent interactions on a personal level to ensure the demand they create is demand they capture, nurture, and guide.

This evolution of the Go to Market approach is good for consumers to connect on a higher level. It's also great for business results. According to at 2019 study by Motista, consumers with an emotional connection to a brand:

- Have a 306 percent higher lifetime value,
- Stay with a brand for an average of 5.1 years vs. 3.4 years,
- Will recommend brands at a much higher rate (71% vs. 45%).

GO TO MARKET APPROACH

The Experience Brand Go to Market approach has, in itself, a series of strategic tenets to keep in mind as it's built and implemented. This requires a different point of view than when approaching traditional acquisition challenges, doing so in a long-term relationship-focused approach, not just a one-and-done transaction. To do this, the Go to Market strategic tenets are:

Retention First

The success of a Go to Market strategy won't necessarily be measured in how much demand (acquisition) it creates, but how much demand it captures, retains and converts (retention). Leading with a retention-first mindset, brands are driven more by the second and third level actions than the first alone. They worry more about onboarding the right consumers into a lifetime relationship than simply getting the next quick sale. They know the true value lies in the repeat purchase, increased loyalty, and recurring revenue—more than in a single transaction. This approach shifts the marketing strategy from a campaign mindset to one that delivers an ecosystem of messaging, interaction, response, and reaction throughout the consumer journey. Retention First requires a brand to create the fly trap of value in the lifestyle of the brand, before any advertising or media is determined.

Capturing demand correctly is a competitive advantage. It allows brands the ability to understand their consumers in more detail, capture consumer data, and use that data along with content, messaging, and media channels to continuously provide new value to the consumer. This use of CRM—media, content, messaging and promotions—gives brands the toolbox needed to engage with and respond to consumers in the best way possible, all personalized on their terms. This approach takes the demand that is created and nurtures it through to a stronger, more valuable relationship between the consumer and the brand, increasing the likelihood of a purchase as well as repeat purchase.

Always-On Demand Creation and Capture

Building on the Experience Brand Strategy, there are opportunities to streamline the research, consideration, shopping, and decision phases of the consumer journey. Traditionally, brands employ an advertising and acquisition approach for their go-to-market strategy by sending out a mass communication to a large audience, hoping that a small percentage of people take action on a purchase. However, Experience Brands, having a retention mindset, use the marketing journey as an opportunity to build an ongoing relationship with their customers over time. By leveraging audience data, behaviors, and context, Experience Brands create an ecosystem of content, messaging, media and calls to action ready to be deployed when the appropriate triggers are hit. This "machine" is built on the idea that demand is created and captured on the consumer's terms, not the brand's—creating a need to be always on and ready when the consumer is. This approach moves the consumer into a continuously running cadence of planned interaction, from the moment they engage with your brand.

Once demand is created, Experience Brands treat their potential customers as if they are already a part of the brand story and narrative with sequential messaging and additional value to guide the relationship toward a purchase.

For example, in the past, for a razor brand, creating breakthrough and acquisition for new product innovation required advertising across mass media channels, hoping the consumer would have brand or product recall when purchasing a new razor at shelf. However, Dollar Shave Club employed a different approach, breaking down the construct of brand/product recall and even the idea of purchasing in a retail store. They led their consumers with a retention-first mindset to employ

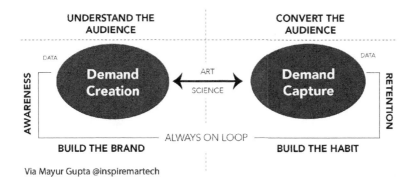

Via Mayur Gupta @inspiremartech

an algorithmic framework to message and guide their consumer toward the brand and, ultimately, a purchase.

Personalization

Consumer expectations have risen to a point of individual personalization. As consumer data is actively captured and used, consumers expect to have a value response from the brands that capture their data. Experience Brands use these expectations and consumer data to create meaningful messages and content to expand the abilities of their Go to Market strategies. They use ownership and interaction data, but they also leverage preference, location, weather, and other various triggers to create a single view of the consumer to best create the right value and the right message, at the right time. This value can take the shape of a message, an offer or promotion, a reduced task, or an expansion of joy.

By connecting the brand value to the consumer's personalized media and content consumption, the brand creates the opportunity for a deeper opt-in than has been possible before. This enables the brand to progressively personalize, to fully understand consumer needs and preferences as they provide them, and to use these elements for the betterment of the relationship.

STRATEGIC FRAMEWORK

A successful Go to Market strategy is a distinct combination of art meeting science. The art is in how the brand intentionally creates the consumer experience, the consumer journey, and the messaging and content that powers it. And the science is in how the creative is targeted and deployed based on audience triggers, context, and interactions. To create and deploy this type of Go to Market strategy requires a revised approach to marketing and what it means for the organization. The most successful Experience Brands integrate consumer-facing business units, functions, and departments into the marketing process to ensure a holistic experience based on a single view of the consumer. Using the assets available at their disposal, they can then go through a strategic development exercise to define the Go to Market framework, and establish the "machine" that runs the strategy.

Change the Incentive

Thinking back to the example at the beginning of this chapter, the goals of sales, while being the necessary outcome, should never be the main goal for a brand's Go to Market strategy. This near-sightedness sends the brand into a reactionary position, which gives into actions that could dilute the brand and value through incorrect messaging, detrimental promotions and incentives or aggressive sales tactics. Instead, brands should understand and always align to the higher purpose of their brand to ensure that as they acquire new customers, they never lose sight of how to treat those customers and how to retain their interest from initial connection through purchase, repurchase, loyalty, and advocacy. When creating a new Go to Market strategy, brands should always plan for a consumer's third purchase versus their first.

Experience Brands operating with a retention-first mindset, have transitioned from campaign metrics to long-term lifetime-value metrics. Instead of just measuring Marketing ROI, Consumer Acquisition Costs, Click Through Rates, and Conversion Percentages, Experience Brands measure Brand and Consumer Value, Engagement and Retention, and Loyalty—metrics that show the brand promise is being fulfilled at moments of interaction while showing the efficiency and effectiveness of their actions.

Strategic Approach

With a renewed sense of goal and obligation, the Go to Market strategy can now be crafted and curated across the entirety of the consumer journey and brand organization. This whole-of-business approach to Go to Market breaks down traditional silos to add increased value to consumers by moving marketing closer to product, to the supply chain, to logistics, and to customer service. This shift creates an organic growth and feedback loop that captures demand in a way that nurtures interest and intent toward, not just a purchase decision, but a lifetime relationship between consumer and brand. This approach allows Experience Brands to have an open dialog with consumers to gather both passive and active feedback along the way, providing much needed insight to the consumer journey for optimization or new value opportunities.

The art part of the Go to Market strategy is defining and intentionally creating the journey the consumer would expect from your brand. Experience Brands are extremely adamant about how their brand comes to life across the consumer journey to ensure it's consistent, progressive, and elicits and fulfills the brand promise with each interaction. There is tremendous power in this intentionality. First, by fully understanding the consumer journey, we understand the expectations, needs and jobs the consumer has. Second, by fully understanding how our Experience Brand should come to life, we can create the interactions, non-interactions, messages, and content to fulfill these expectations, needs and jobs in a way that only our brand can.

The science aspect of this type of Go to Market strategy is the "Machine" that runs the experience. This includes the audience details and data, the CRM system that captures and leverages this data, the algorithms that act as the decision-making layer, the analytics that trigger context and behavior, the marketing technology that deploys the creative and message, and the receivers that take consumer interaction, preference, and behavioral data to create a new experience. As we'll see next, these elements will be strategically designed using the "art" or creativity from the brand perspective and will be implemented using the "science" or technology aspect of the organization. Experience Brands deploy their Go to Market activities at this intersection of brand strategy and technology to ensure that consistent, progressive relationships are being established, at scale.

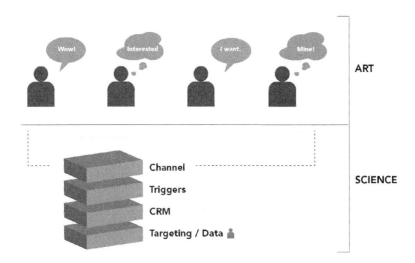

THE MACHINE

Strategic Development

The Go to Market machine may conjure up images of Robbie the Robot screaming "Danger Will Robinson," but that couldn't be farther from the truth. In fact, the machine we're talking about here is a series of processes, algorithms, and analytics that connect the consumer journey with the right messages, content, interactions, and hand-offs from the brand to create the highest value possible in this symbiotic brand-consumer relationship. Let's face it, consumers who buy from you are looking to buy a product or service similar to yours, so your Go to Market strategy should connect these dots as easily and with as much value as possible. This is where the "machine" makes it work.

Consumer Journey Map

Fully understanding the journey a consumer takes to do business with your brand or to purchase a product or service like the ones you sell, gives you tremendous power in determining the right channels, devices, messages, content, and experiences your brand needs to create in order to streamline the purchase process and create the value needed to engage your customer. A detailed and progressive consumer journey map provides the blueprint for critical opportunities to maximize your Go to Market strategy and to enable your machine.

Interaction Points: The first things you'll notice in your consumer journey map are the interaction points. These are the moments, places, channels, and devices where and when consumers are actively or passively interacting with brands in your industry when trying to solve a problem— their "jobs to be done." These points could range from a Google search, to a website visit, to an in-store visit, or to scheduling an appointment. The interaction points should be used to convey and fulfill your brand promise while providing expected and incremental value to the consumer. This could be eliminating actions, easing the process, providing the right information, or even as simple as giving them a great message based on their personal history with your brand. Each of these interaction points comes with a tremendous opportunity. They give your brand a chance to ensure that the interaction is valuable, and they also have the ability to capture data to inform subsequent interaction points.

Data Capture Opportunities: Data capture is, and will always be, a contentious point in marketing, as it should be. Companies should not have the ability to manipulate or use data in any derogatory or unethical way. It should be used only to add value for the consumer. When Seth Godin wrote about Permission Marketing in 1999, we, as marketers, witnessed a behavioral shift in how to market to consumers. The stakes have drastically increased in the time since then and the idea of permission marketing has expanded into attention. In today's marketplace, brands must continuously vie for the attention of consumers with other brands that have gained "permission" to talk to them. However, the best way to stand out in this crowded world is to capture and use data in the most meaningful and valuable way. Use consumer interaction and preference to customize your services and products. Create a personalized experience just for them. With the technology and data capture we have at our disposal; we should be doing more to add value to our consumers.

Moments of Chore or Joy: When going through your consumer journey map, interaction points and data capture opportunities, you can layer on consumer sentiment to better understand the mindset and attitude of the consumer at a particular point in the process. This information allows you to know which interaction points are painful and which one's spark joy. You can almost look at this from a quadrant perspective. On the x axis you can have the spectrum of pain to joy. On the y axis you can determine if the interaction is necessary or can be eliminated. This process is ripe with opportunity and economic value for your brand. By removing the painful and unnecessary chores and expanding on the necessary and joyful moments, you can completely transform your brand in the marketplace.

Competitive Analysis: To take this a step further to ensure you are consistently creating competitive value in the marketplace, you can even layer on the activities competitors do at a specific interaction point. Unfortunately, there are actions and interactions that consumers feel they have to perform in order to make a decision, that if you found it as a pain point and your brand didn't have that action, you would be dismissed immediately. An example of this is a Build and Price tool for auto manufacturers. It is a cumbersome process that consumers really don't enjoy, but if a brand removed it, it wouldn't be able to communicate the right information to the consumer and the brand would be removed from the consideration set.

Data and Targeting

Data is the lifeblood of the Go to Market machine. It is used to best target audiences that your brand is trying to affect, but gathered and enhanced through the interaction, conversion, analytic, preference, and personal data that consumers offer to provide. All of these data points can be used to grow your brand and maximize your Go to Market strategy, if used correctly. Identifying these data sets and making them accessible and usable is a great first step; acting on the data is where creativity and art take over to bring the true power to life.

Algorithm and Trigger Development

Using the consumer journey map, the insight around which chores to remove and which interaction points to expand, and the data available, we have the foundation to develop our engagement and re-engagement opportunities for the Go to Market strategy. By understanding the jobs consumers are trying to solve at any given moment in time, we can build a messaging and engagement cadence, fueled by data, and managed by algorithms. These algorithms and triggers are developed with brand defined scenario planning and recipes, coupled with consumer data, interactions, and behaviors. These algorithms or recipes are simple "if this then that" scenarios that we can establish to trigger a focused interaction or the guidance and rules for subsequent interactions or non-interactions. These algorithms allow you to capture and use data accordingly throughout the consumer journey and the consumer experience. Planning out the entirety of the Go to Market strategy against the consumer journey map and the Experience Brand strategy will give you the insight needed to build the right cadence, engagement tactics, messaging, content, and conversion measures.

Content and Messaging Development

Now that the machine is strategically designed, the data is usable and actionable, the algorithms are defined and the channels connected, we can get into creative development. Content Strategies are built with the idea of audience type and need, their job to be done, and the active and passive inputs from the consumer journey. This will allow us to build a context-focused dynamic-messaging framework, that can be activated according to plan, or pivot based on changing consumer needs.

Audience and Persona Development: Understanding the audience nuance, even down to the individual, is the most important aspect of winning as an Experience Brand. Not only do you understand their pain points and moments of joy, but you also understand the channels and devices they frequent, the content they consume, the detailed demographic and psychographic information, but also the preferences and sentiment regarding brands, products, and services in and around your industry. You start to get a sense of their experience expectations as they navigate through other brands and industries. Creating an audience framework that allows you to start at high level segments, then work down to definitive tribes and even to individuals, we can build out detailed personas that give us a starting point to develop content and messaging.

Content Strategy: One thing is certain; a mass-media approach doesn't succeed in the Journey Economy. We need to understand the consumer point of view, then serve the right content in the right channel at the right time to garner the right context. By understanding the consumer personas in detail, we can create a framework for content and messaging. Building on the Jobs to be Done at certain touchpoints, on certain channels, and with certain mind-states, we can create the right content to be molded to solve the consumer challenge. The content strategy will combine the consumer jobs with the brand strategy to create the highest probability for engagement. Each content artifact or object should be used for the purpose of solving the consumer challenge in hopes of moving them toward the next brand conversion. Remember, Experience Brands build for the second and third interactions, based on scenarios; these come to life through content strategy, with responsive messages, and a call to action.

Content needs, artifacts, and cadence will be determined based on the audience needs and expectations as well as the channels with which they engage. Content needs to be customized for the audience, connecting expectations to brand promise or features. It also should follow the best practices of the channel where the content is being consumed. Not only that, but the content strategy should become progressive, based on messaging cadence, interactions, and accessible consumer profile data. These elements create the most powerful approach for a Go to Market strategy but also build on the objective of a retention-first mindset.

To put it in terms of the day, the reality of the content strategy will be a combination of brand content and performance-based marketing. This creates the overarching lifestyle that needs to be established for a retention-first mindset, while deploying the action-oriented content to guide the consumer to convert—whether capturing data, tracking an interaction, signing up for more information, or even making a purchase. This strategic balance of brand content and performance-based marketing creates a holistic brand experience for the consumer to engage with throughout their journey, even if it's the first time they are interacting with your brand.

Messaging Framework: Understanding the content strategy you can quickly move into production, deployment, and optimization. Messaging should be used to either start or continue a dialog your brand wants to have with the consumer, knowing that the consumer pain point is truly what you must solve for. The messaging framework in this go-to-market approach must be dynamic to cater to the progressive needs of the strategy. While the messaging has to include baseline job-to-be-done messaging, it should also have the sequential messages created that ease the consumer journey from one point to another. Once the consumer interacts with or continues to opt in to further permission, the messaging framework should allow for personalization and preference-led messaging.

Messaging is crucial in the Experience Brand strategy as it is the direct thing that consumers learn from and interact with throughout their journey. Whether it's a long form piece of content, a voice response from Alexa, or a referral from a friend, the way that messages are crafted has to appeal to the individual on their level but also have the portability and scalability across channel, medium or device, whether direct or indirect. Creating this type of messaging framework, you need to have a story arc from the brand that builds the ideal relationship with the consumer, but also has the dynamic ability to sequence, personalize, pivot, or even walk away if it's not a right fit.

Role of Media

As brands start to live and participate in an Experience Brand world in regard to the Go to Market strategy, the perception of media shifts completely. The goals shift from acquisition to engagement and retention. The channels evolve from mostly mass media, to more-personalized, behavioral-driven platforms. The approach shifts from a one-way message to true, two-way relationships based on consumer interactions and intentions. This manifests into a media mix and messaging that evolves based on how a specific consumer segment or consumer interacts with the brand and message. Paid media is used to scale the organic growth approach that we've established throughout this section.

Scaling for Experience Brands requires looking at media spends and strategy across various teams within an organization. Not only do you need to understand how to drive new consumers into the funnel, but once you understand the consumer behavior and needs, you need to be able to shift the media mix to respond. There may be a time where a consumer purchases on the first message, or a current owner needs service and loyalty messaging, or a consumer just started his or her search for a product. This is where the journey comes into play and the alignment between business units is crucial for success. The role that media plays in a platform world is based on the consumer need, not the business need. Organizations need to act accordingly.

Tech Stack

Now that strategic development, or "art," of The Machine is in place, you need to implement the technology stack, or "science," that seamlessly and repeatedly executes against these strategic rules. The tech stack is built to target the audience appropriately, serve the right content, capture active and inactive data, respond based on the decision matrices through algorithms, and then, finally, measure and optimize the entire journey. The Machine tech stack automates what can be automated and hands off to a human when the trigger deems necessary.

Targeting & Data Aggregation

Creating a unified view of the consumer through targeting has proven to be a near impossibility with off-the-shelf technology. Not only do walled gardens like Facebook, Google, and Apple hold onto their data, but browser-based tracking is quickly going away, furthering the challenges faced by marketers. However, there is hope on the horizon. There are companies and technologies like Amperity that are able to leverage and unify consumer profiles to be acted against. This means that the first-party customer data you have in your CRM and the consumer profile data in social media channels and on their personal devices can be matched and acted upon in a "clean room" of sorts. It gives marketers the power to aggregate, leverage, and build upon consumer profiles across walled gardens to gain a singular view of consumers. This becomes the fuel of your Go to Market tech stack.

Customer Relationship Management

The most valuable asset your company has is the relationship you build with each individual customer. By knowing and understanding them on an individual basis, you can offer up products, services, and experiences that are personalized and best suited for their lifestyles. In return, they become more loyal to your brand and your cause. This is where the retention-first mindset comes into play. The success of these individual relationships is dependent on your customer relationship management system (CRM). By leveraging a dynamic CRM like Salesforce, brands and businesses can implement their Go to Market strategies that build and expand consumer profiles, progressively understanding the consumer more as an individual. This first-party data becomes the lifeblood of the Go to Market strategy and the growth of the business in the long run.

Deploying Algorithms and Triggers

Now that you can target, capture and access the data needed to best engage and understand your consumers, you'll need to implement the decision-making rules to execute the Go to Market strategy. These rules will be built on top of the CRM as "if this, then that" scenarios to trigger channels, content, messaging, and promotions to solve the consumer challenges while fulfilling the brand's Go to Market strategy. To get a sense of light touch "recipes," I urge you to look at IFTTT. com or Zapier. They are productivity platforms that have made it easy to create trigger-based algorithms that take an input (trigger) and execute a recipe. For example, if you get an email from a certain contact on Gmail, you can automatically trigger a response on Twitter. To scale these up, enterprise SaaS (software as a service) companies like Salesforce allow you to take your decision trees and make them into algorithms on your CRM, deployed across your marketing and commerce channels.

Channel Activation

It is crucial for your data, CRM and algorithms to work across channels as one orchestrated strategy. If it doesn't, you risk breaking the consumer journey and experience, not capturing vital consumer data, and you could even miss out on the ability to attribute certain tactics to conversions. The term interoperability applies here; or the ability for your Go to Market Machine to seamlessly work across channels and allow for data to pass back and forth. By using tools like Google's DoubleClick for digital advertising, Buffer for social publishing, and Salesforce for CRM, your tech stack can be synchronized to effectively activate your channels according to your content and messaging strategy, all while passing analytics and consumer data back to the brand to capture and continue to act upon.

MEASUREMENT AND OPTIMIZATION

The ongoing success of this Go to Market approach and the established Go to Market Machine is driven by the ability to continually monitor, measure, and optimize. By using the consumer journey map as the foundational benchmark for the consumer, your brand, and your competition at certain touchpoints, you will have a tremendous view of the marketplace and your consumer. You will be able to see where bottlenecks form, where pain points start or end, and how to better optimize and test your content and messaging strategies.

WINNING WITH GO TO MARKET

Experience Brands have a completely different mindset when it comes to advertising, marketing, and Go to Market activities. They focus beyond the initial acquisition and into retention. This retention-first mindset gives Experience Brands the latitude to act differently earlier in the consumer relationship, which adds more value to the brand itself, making it more appealing to purchase and engage with. Thus, the Experience Brand Go to Market strategy is rooted in capturing and nurturing the demand that is created in a relationship development strategy, versus acquisition. This always-on approach intentionally creates demand, then transfers that demand into conversions across the value exchanges throughout the consumer journey.

The strategic framework for the Go to Market strategy creates a new perspective on demand creation. It intentionally creates the metrics and key performance indicators aligned with a retention-first mindset where the brand activity leads with the lifestyle first and acquisition second. The combination of brand messaging and performance-based marketing is the driving force for a holistic view of the consumer experience as it relates to generating the demand needed to capture, nurture, and convert into members of the brand, versus simply someone buying from you.

The Go to Market strategy is powered by a robust and dynamic marketing machine, built to automatically run the plays needed to fulfill your Experience Brand strategy in the acquisition part of the consumer journey. The machine itself is a combination of the overarching strategic development of brand messaging with performance-based marketing leading to building relationships with individual consumers, welcoming and onboarding them into the brand lifestyle. Once established, the machine strategy is enabled through the development and implementation of technology. The tech stack is used to power the algorithms, which trigger content, messaging, and experience based on the strategy and the consumer profile data.

The ultimate goal of the Go to Market strategy is moving the consumer toward a purchase decision. However, the personalization that comes along with it leads into a dynamic commerce strategy, a robust service and loyalty experience and, progressively, into new value within the business model itself.

www.JourneyEconomy.com/chapter-7

#gotomarket@PaulMiser

LESSONS LEARNED

- Experience Brands think retention first, serving the customers on a deeper, more personalized level. Once the retention mindset is established, demand and acquisition come more easily.
- The integration of brand advertising and performance marketing connects demand creation with a systematic demand-capture strategy. Experience Brands build the

lifestyle that captures the demand in a way that is continuously valuable to their consumer.

- This demand creation and demand capture is executed using a marketing Machine. On the front-end it's the strategic development: consumer journey, database development algorithm recipes, content, messaging, and media. On the backend, it's the tech stack that brings it to life: the database, the algorithms, the channel development, and the digital products and platforms that enable the capturing and nurturing of demand, based on the Experience Brand strategy.

- Remaining agile and knowing when to optimize, pivot, or walk away from a strategy is crucial to the success of an Experience Brand Go to Market strategy.

CHAPTER 8

ANYTIME, ANYWHERE COMMERCE

RETAIL ISN'T DEAD, IT'S JUST DIFFERENT

"The three most important things in retail are location, location, location. The three most important things for our consumer business are technology, technology, technology."

Jeff Bezos

THE NEXT action expands upon the Go To Market strategy and is built on the shifting expectations of commerce. From a consumer's perspective, commerce isn't brick and mortar versus e-commerce versus mobile. It's a personalized journey where their preferences and decisions progressively follow them across screen, device, and aisle. Experience Brands are establishing the frameworks to connect commerce channels together by consumer behavior, and also provide transaction opportunities on the consumer's terms, not the brand's. With this approach, commerce and transactions become a competitive differentiator for brands as they connect the entirety of the experience.

"With 30 percent of e-commerce sales coming from recommendations, the case for personalization is clear. The same is true with anywhere commerce, since 75 percent of shopping behavior begins online. The experience of retail is changing because of tech."
Satya Nadella, CEO, Microsoft

RETAIL BEHAVIORS AND TRENDS

Retail isn't dead. It's just different. The challenge isn't finding new ways for consumers to spend more, it's about being there when they are ready to spend. And by "being there" a brand needs to have an always-on commerce strategy that works cross device and cross channel. Commerce isn't a brick and mortar versus e-commerce decision. It's brick and mortar AND e-commerce, AND social commerce, AND marketplace, AND recurring transactions. Experience Brands understand the consumer journey intimately to know when and where they need to be in order to provide a transaction moment.

Experience Brands also know what needs to happen to ease a transaction and change it from a pain point into a moment of cherish. That is, to be as personalized as possible. As consumers shop and decide what they want to purchase they usually use multiple channels and mediums. The decisions they've made, the items they've placed in their baskets and their preferences need to follow them to the moment of transaction, wherever that may be. The decisions, interactions, and preferences captured in the Go to Market strategy can now be used to guide consumers through a transaction, wherever they may be.

For example, if you're a sportswear company that sells products on e-commerce, in your own stores, and through third-party retailers, you want to make sure you are maximizing revenue and profits while fulfilling your brand for your consumers, regardless of channel. Your consumer, on the other hand, wants the best product to up their game in the easiest way possible. As we'll see in an Experience Brand Profile, Nike has employed an omni-channel commerce strategy that puts the consumer in the center of the experience. By creating a value-based mobile application, Nike has built a single view of its consumers that can translate from channel to channel—digital to physical. The mobile app includes functionality that connects the sport with product and content; connects product with shopping; and connects preference and product with the retailer. This provides the consumer with a new way to learn about, shop for, try, and purchase products on their terms, raising the probability for purchase and increased basket size.

NEW RETAIL

Tying everything together is where success in retail lies. Each channel—e-commerce, brick and mortar, third-party retailers, or marketplace—needs to work in concert to ensure a seamless, personalized experience and provide ready-to-purchase moments. Experience Brands are breaking down the internal silos of commerce to create a singular experience for the consumer. Whether it's new agreements with third-party retailers or their direct-to-consumer teams or owned brick and mortar technologies, Experience Brands enable their channels to best service the consumer.

E-commerce Brands build commerce into all interactions to make the purchase seamless and effortless for the consumer, ready for when the consumer is. This commerce strategy breaks down the walls of traditional thinking of e-commerce versus brick and mortar and into the value these channels can have if they work together. As we'll see in the case studies, traditional transactions are becoming archaic as the power of the transaction is in the hands of the consumer.

On the Go

Mobile technology has completely changed the behaviors of shoppers. Not only are they in an always-on shopping mode, but they are using their phones in physical stores to get deeper information, compare prices, and even purchase products. I remember, from 2010 until 2019, tech gurus would constantly claim that each year would be the year in which mobile overtakes all shopping. It wasn't until Black Friday 2018 in the U.S. when this prediction became a reality. In fact, it is estimated that in 2021, mobile commerce will become 54 percent of total e-commerce sales, leaving brands with the challenge of integrating a commerce ecosystem that truly puts consumers, and their devices, at the center. However, this increase doesn't make mobile a "channel" we should focus on and optimize, but rather a conduit for delivering a personalized and holistic experience, putting our assets in the right roles together, not competing against each other.

Personalization

Consumers expect brands to listen to them and respond accordingly. Now, as more and more transactions are blending online and offline, consumers expect brands to transfer those interactions from channel to channel, building a progressive understanding of their decisions, preferences, and needs, picking up a conversation where they left off. This personal-ization builds trust, and also guides the consumer through a purchase more quickly. Personalization strategies are enabled through customer data capturing and management tools, CRM platforms, and commerce platforms.

Product-izing Transaction

The way that consumers transact in today's business environment is more important than ever before. Whether it's replacing a traditional transaction with e-commerce or a a single purchase with a subscription, consumers are looking to companies to innovate the way they tactically do business with them, while adding value to the brand-consumer relationship. For example, the company Dirty Lemon, which makes lemonade-based wellness drinks, has completely innovated the way consumers transact with their products. Instead of going through a traditional grocery or convenience store purchase, they are opening self-serve kiosks in high-traffic locations, such as Hudson Yards in New York City, where the consumer just picks a product, scans a QR code, and walks away, drastically reducing the transaction pain points. Amazon Go stores are another example of productizing the transaction to ensure the biggest pain point in a purchase (the physical purchase itself) is removed. By looking at transactions as a product in and of itself, Experience Brands have the ability to offer products, services, and brands that are ready to be distributed or consumed in the best, most valuable way.

APPROACH: ANYTIME, ANYWHERE COMMERCE

The evolution of retail, and commerce in general, is the con-cept of "Anytime, Anywhere" commerce. This is providing continued value for the consumer throughout the shop, buy, and own journey across aisle, screen or device, connecting each consumer with what matters most to them individually. This approach gives brands the opportunity to use shopping, transaction, and consumption moments as elements of their continued Experience Brand story. Building on the trends outlined above, crafting your "Anytime, Anywhere Commerce" strategy begins where your consumer's behavior and needs intersect with your Experience Brand strategy.

Experience Brands are rewriting the boundaries of what retail strategy looks like by breaking down the traditional silos and recreating their organizations to support the consumer experience. Connection is the lifeblood of Anytime, Anywhere Commerce. By leveraging consumer journeys, Experience Brands understand the role that each commerce channel plays in the shopping and purchasing process for the consumer and at what time. Connecting experience with channels puts the consumer in the center of the purchase cycle, which is exactly where they should be. An example of this is the Rebecca Minkoff store in New York. They leverage the use of smart mirrors to connect the trial experience to their unified consumer profile. This allows a shopper to shop online, put things in their basket, transition to a store and "log in," put more things in their fitting room, then simply go to the fitting room to try the products on. This orchestrated experience is a combination of platform, data, process, and the people in the store, to facilitate the capturing of interest and the result of trial in a fitting room.

ROLES OF COMMERCE

Implementing the commerce strategy with the various elements will require an understanding of the channels, how they fit into the Experience Brand strategy, how data can be captured and utilized, and how to best connect the dots to create a seamless experience. The different commerce channels all have pros and cons, but each channel should have a definitive primary, secondary and tertiary role in the entirety of the consumer journey. These roles should also be based on the audience development and persona work that was done to map the consumer journey. Understanding the nuance by audience will increase the effectiveness of the strategy.

Brick and Mortar has been positioned as the dying dinosaur in all of business. According to Coresight Research, a record 9,500 retail stores went out of business in 2019 and as many as 25,000 could shut down permanently in 2020, mostly in malls. And with stats like this, one can get down on the role of brick and mortar. As we mentioned at the start of this chapter, retail isn't dead, it's just different. In many industries, brick and mortar still plays a vital role for consumers. Brick and Mortar offers several benefits for the consumer. Not only does brick and mortar provide an innate ability for happenstance in exploration, but also the ability for product trial, immediate gratification, in-person support, and the human desire for impulse. For those industries and companies with high-consideration purchases like cars, mattresses, or consumer electronics there is a high proportion of consumers who still want to touch, feel, and try a product and its features before they purchase. This is a massive opportunity for brands to execute their Experience Brand strategies at these key moments, but not treat them as a silo by themselves.

Sales Support is when your sales force is empowered with more information about a customer, prospect or lead. By giving them information like shopping behaviors, cart items, product preferences, interactions and content consumption, the salesperson becomes more informed about the specific needs of the individual person. This allows them to create a more customized or personalized approach when interacting with and communicating with the consumer. This enhances the experience the consumer has, while also generating a stronger bond through your human resources. However, once the interaction with the salesperson is over, the data, insight and information that was generated in those interactions, must be integrated into the CRM to aggregate all information on the individual consumer to support the next interaction, wherever she may interact.

E-commerce has quickly grown into the primary source of sale for many consumer demographics across many different industries, with even larger, more complex purchases like mattresses and cars making the transition. In fact, 16 percent of all retail sales in the U.S. were through e-commerce with an estimated 25 percent of all retail sales being e-commerce by 2025. E-commerce is basically leveraging technology to allow for a transaction to happen online. This powers websites and marketplaces and, as we'll see below, the rise of mobile and social commerce. This has also generated an opportunity for brick and mortar stores to use e-commerce transactions, in a physical location. The great thing about e-commerce is its simplicity in the transaction, its personalization in being connected to data and preference, and its permeability by having the ability to travel from site to site, device to device, and location to location. E-commerce has become a massive transformation for many companies and, rather than integrating with their current platforms, they have built separate business units to support the growth, acting in a silo from the rest of the commerce teams. Experience Brands on the other hand have folded this transaction into the broader shop, buy, own, service model and have found ways to leverage its unique ability for compounded success.

Mobile Commerce (m-commerce)—built on e-commerce—has become a leading force in how consumers are choosing to transact. Mobile purchases have doubled in the last five years to 45 percent of the total e-commerce sales. Mobile commerce has the unique ability to be an extension of the consumer, knowing all personal information and preference, being there right at the moment of insight and, more and more, having the transaction methods stored on the device. The technological advances that have brought mobile commerce to the forefront are continuing to expand, increasing the role of mobile in all transactions. Technologies like ApplePay, RFID, and WePay have led to the mobile device becoming the central element in many transactions across industry for the consumer. Experience Brands are leveraging this trend to create more connected experiences. Companies like Nike, Amazon and adidas are using m-commerce to create mobile-specific experiences, but also opening the value and technology of mobile to expand and extend other experiences in their commerce ecosystem, like brick and mortar.

Social Commerce is experiencing gains in popularity and exposure of late. The success of retail or commerce is to be able to have your product or service and offer in front of the consumer at the moment of insight. Nowadays, a lot of those moments of insight are happening in the social scroll, where consumers are finding the products and services in their streams of content. Platforms like Instagram have begun integrating transactions and commerce on the platform itself, so as consumers find what they want, they can transact then and there without leaving the platform. Social Commerce plays the role of both awareness and impulse. Depending on the impulsiveness of their product or service, Experience Brands use Social Commerce as the culture-forward abstraction of their brand, bringing people into the brand and a purchase quickly through connection and content.

Marketplaces, like Amazon and Walmart (building on the back of ebay) have taken the industry by storm. Not only do they offer a direct e-commerce platform, but they also allow third parties to sell products on their platforms to get scale and consumer access. These marketplaces have not only created massive leverage for the platforms but have also increased the opportunity for competition and noise for the consumer. This has resulted in some pretty frightening behavioral shifts among consumers for brands to overcome. For example, 70 percent of all searches on Amazon are for generic products, not brand names. This means that in order to break through, brands must own the generic search and provide the value on the marketplace to capture the mind of consumers as they are searching for your product, but not your brand. What has happened is that brands can do one of two things, embrace the marketplace platforms and leverage them as a valuable asset, or try to compete with the marketplace search to generate brand awareness, engagement and transaction prior to the consumer going to the marketplaces.

BRINGING IT TO LIFE

Building on the Experience Brand strategy and the Go to Market strategy, we are now in a position to bring the commerce strategy to life to streamline, ease, and expand purchase behaviors from consumers. Experience Brands have a unique ability to create transactions as welcomed experiences across aisle, screens and device, seamlessly connecting consumer preferences with products and with a transaction opportunity, all where and how the consumer wants to purchase—unlike traditional companies, where consumers are forced into a transaction process built on business operations, not consumer wants and needs.

Commerce Ecosystem

The first step in implementing an Experience Brand commerce strategy is to define your brand's commerce ecosystem. This is mapping out what channels resonate with your audience segments, understanding why they resonate and ultimately what consumers want those channels to do for them in their purchase journey. The next step is to figure out what information or preferences consumers expect or want to have passed through each channel or platform. The goal with connecting the retail ecosystem is to become as valuable to the consumer as possible, easing the transaction for a seamless purchase from their journey to that point. Not all brands will leverage all channels, but most will use a combination of e-commerce, brick and mortar, and sales support. Examples of Experience Brand Commerce Ecosystems can be found in the Experience Brand Profile section at the end of this Chapter. Nike, Amazon, and Warby Parker have been using new technologies, consumer profile information and audience-specific channels to best support, guide, and engage their consumers to, through, and after the purchase.

Channel Development

With the channels defined for the commerce ecosystem, the next step is getting them set up to work as stand-alone or together, based on the needs and expectations of the consumer. Using the consumer journey and unified customer profile work we established earlier in the process, we can now set out to establish and connect the dots of the commerce ecosystem through data and device of the audience segments.

Experience Brands use the behaviors and interactions from one channel to pass on to the next. For example, if your customers have been shopping online, even putting things in their carts brands are passing that personal and interaction data into other channels, like brick and mortar or to mobile commerce. The ability to have a consumer profile is crucial for success at this stage in the consumer journey, which is why the Go to Market strategy is extremely important to get right, before embarking on a Commerce strategy.

As mentioned above, women's fashion brand Rebecca Minkoff has blended its channels in a completely immersive way. While the consumer shops online or even in a store, smart features like mirrors in the store allow the consumer to personalize their experience as they shop. They can add things to their cart, which translates to their profile in the store for a fitting room or to checkout. The seamless interaction from digital to physical and back to digital is creating a deeper relationship with their consumers as they increase the value throughout the shopping and transaction activity.

Integration

The ultimate goal for becoming an Experience Brand is to continuously add value in the relationship consumers have with your brand. The best way to do this is to progressively understand the expectations of your consumers and then use the data and information you have about them in a valuable way at each touchpoint. This is only expanded at moments of commerce and transaction. By learning about and using data in their commerce strategy, brands can turn the thought of transactions and purchases from a negative element in the consumer journey, into something exciting, fulfilling, and rewarding. Too often, traditional brands create transaction environments that are cold, emotionless and, overtly bene-fit the brand, not the consumer. Experience Brands, on the other hand, use transactions as a moment to connect on a personal level with the customers by using their preferences and expectations as drivers for welcoming them into the brand experience and the brand lifestyle. They use these moments to start the next level of relationship, that of member in their brand. They don't just transact and walk away like many traditional brands. Experience Brands use personalization to start preparing for the next transaction in a progressive, relationship-driven way.

• • •

EXPERIENCE BRAND PROFILE: NIKE
Connecting Consumers – Digital & Physical

Nike is pushing the boundaries in Anytime, Anywhere Commerce with several initiatives. From immersive retail experiences to integrated purchasing across Instagram and other social channels, Nike has established a foundation for cross channel purchase success.

However, the Nike App at Retail is what is truly revolutionary. The app supports mobile, owned physical retail and third-party retail in a seamless, brand-forward way, giving the power to shop and buy to consumers when they are ready.

Nike at Owned Retail: Nike has used the power of technology to support the in-store shopping experience. When customers use the Nike app, Nike gains access to the consumer's profile. This opens up a world of opportunity:

- **Scan and Shop:** The consumer can scan a product and get deeper information or get a size brought out to them.
- **Ask Questions:** Consumers can chat with and summon sales associates for help.
- **Prepare a Fitting Room:** Consumers can scan products and add their size to a fitting room.
- **Check out:** Once done shopping, consumers can check out directly from their app and leave the store; no checkout line, no transaction.

Nike Connecting Digital with Physical: Using some of the same functionality as in-store, consumers can shop on their app and have the physical store react.

- **Prepare the fitting room:** Consumers can schedule a fitting room appointment with products they like.
- **Place on Hold:** Consumers can place items on hold to ensure the store has their size ready for them.
- **Purchase and Pickup**: Consumers can purchase on their phone and pickup in store.

Nike at Third Party Retail: Using the connected shopping app and consumer profile, Nike has established relationships with their third-party retailers to support functionality with their store point-of-sale systems. Many of the functions described above can also be supported in these stores.

"The way we look at digital and in-store is not channel-by-channel, or one channel helping the other. Instead, we architected the entire notion of why someone with a phone in their pocket would walk into a store. We want to have the best store experience where our most connected customers are, whereas another company might look at the inverse — if people are shopping in the app, they don't need a store there. But we see our approach as better serving our customers."

Michael Martin, Global Head of Digital Products, Nike

• • •

EXPERIENCE BRAND PROFILE: WARBY PARKER
Shifting a Category through New Behaviors

Warby Parker has built its brand on challenging convention by providing products and services that surround the consumer. This comes to life in the way they've built their commerce strategy. They defined the pain points with shopping for and purchasing eyewear. Starting with in-home trials, they built a data-driven approach to knowing their customers' preferences, needs, and wants and then expanded outward.

They built and launched shopping technologies that eliminated certain eye tests and allowed the user to "virtually" try on frames before ordering. Their approach to physical retail started by using e-commerce and website data to launch a pop-up retail tour with a school bus, continuing to track consumer interest and preference before investing in brick and mortar.

"The brand is not just the product, it's the moment someone hears the name 'Warby Parker.'"

Neil Blumenthal

BRINGING YOUR COMMERCE STRATEGY TO ANYTIME, ANYWHERE

As we've seen, retail isn't dead, it's just different. Instead of channel against channel and pressure-based sales situations, we're seeing brands shift their mindset toward a value-driven experience. By connecting and integrating elements in the shopping and transaction part of the consumer journey, Experience Brands are intentionally creating new value by becoming more relevant, more contextual and more personalized as the consumer moves across screen, device, and aisle. This approach offers up the ability for Anytime, Anywhere Commerce, giving consumers the power to seamlessly purchase items, services, or experiences on their terms, based on their personal interaction with the brand.

This approach, again, puts an emphasis on the consumer journey and the value created within that journey through brand interactions. As you mapped out in your consumer journey mapping exercise and defined in your Experience Brand strategy, the moment of transaction and commerce turns into an invitation or welcome into the lifestyle your brand creates. Using personalization to ease the pain points traditionally found at these moments, Experience Brands create a deeper, more trusting connection that transforms the transaction into something cherished.

Experience Brands live and breathe the mindset that the transaction is only the beginning of the relationship. The trust that is built throughout the consumer journey up to this point is merely a promise from the brand that needs to be fulfilled. Any leader of an Experience Brand will tell you that what you do once a purchase is made is where the true return comes into play—the lifetime value of the consumer relationship. As the transaction subsides, the real work of servicing, building satisfaction, creating loyalty, and driving repurchase and advocacy begins.

www.JourneyEconomy.com/chapter-8

#commerce@PaulMiser

LESSONS LEARNED

- The New Retail environment is one where brands have to add value to the consumer to and through a purchase; across screen, device, and aisle, all while making the experience as personalized as possible.
- Experience Brands enable an Anytime, Anywhere Commerce strategy to ensure they build their organization and channels around the consumer experience, not around the different business units within the organization. This strategy is seamless to the consumer and is used to ease the transaction, while gaining more valuable data to pass onto the service and loyalty aspects of the relationship.
- Understanding the roles of each channel that makes up the Commerce Strategy, puts things in perspective for brand and the consumer. Passing the right data and information to and through the different channels will meet consumer expectations and add new value to the consumer through the purchase transaction.

- Again, Experience Brands lean on the consumer journey map and the unified consumer profile to activate the Anytime, Anywhere Commerce strategy—putting role to channel, meeting consumer expectations, passing on data and preferences, and using technology to bring the strategy to life.

CHAPTER 9

MEMBERSHIP

RELATIONSHIPS TO CREATE AND EXPAND A LIFESTYLE

"When the customer comes first, the customer will last."
Robert Half

THROUGHOUT my career, I've noticed that many organizations are set up in two broad categories: marketing, and sales and service. Marketing is meant to bring in new customers, while sales and service is meant to convert the customers and service them during their time of ownership. On the surface, this sounds like a great way to be structured. However, the reality is that in large, complex organizations these two departments or functions rarely talk to each other, creating a broken experience for the consumer and missed opportunities for the brand. Marketing has the ability to prepare consumers for transaction and ownership while establishing an ongoing relationship with the consumer. Sales and service has the ability to understand ownership, consumption, and loyalty—information that could be leveraged by marketing to continue the relationship beyond purchase and into something bigger.

One of the biggest factors in the success and exponential growth of Experience Brands is the way they retain customers and expand demand and purchase moments. Doing this continuously adds value to the brand, while creating more opportunity to invest in the experience for the consumer, increasing the value the consumer receives along the way. These factors are driven by the Experience Brand mindset of retention and membership. Many traditional organizations end the relationship upon purchase, only to be engaged again when things go wrong during ownership or when it's time to repurchase a product.

Experience Brands, on the other hand, use the purchase as the starting point to a longer-term relationship with their consumers. By using the preferences and the information they have gathered on the consumer throughout the Go to Market and Commerce journeys, Experience Brands welcome customers as new members into the brand's lifestyle. They create customized onboarding processes, ask for feedback, are proactive with tips and tricks for the items and services the consumer purchased, and they continuously find ways to add value in the post purchase, membership relationship. These efforts not only increase the probability of repurchase, but also increase the subsequent basket sizes and rates of loyalty and advocacy.

In the Journey Economy, ownership is transforming into membership. Loyalty is transforming into empathy. Advocacy is transforming into relationship.

OPERATIONAL BRANDING

To enable the shift from an ownership to a membership mindset, Experience Brands implement what's called "Operational Branding," where everything in their organization ladders up to an overarching Experience Brand strategy. This approach ensures that each interaction a consumer has with the brand, from research, to shopping, to buying, to customer support, creates the same experience and feelings for the consumer. Far too often, traditional brands working in siloed organizations, have fragmented experiences when the consumer goes from crisp and clear advertising, to a broken website, a dirty retail store, or a poor customer support experience. Implementing Operational Branding measures ensures that the processes, personnel, and operational elements of the company are communicating and interacting the same way for the consumer, post purchase.

Experience Brands also look beyond a single acquisition and know that the true value of acquisition is retention and lifetime value. The first acquisition is just the entry into the lifetime relationship between the brand and the consumer. This mindset gives Experience Brands the foresight to define and deliver the post-purchase elements that keep the consumer engaged with the brand to ensure satisfaction and loyalty. Building this relationship creates opportunities to add value, all leading toward a repeat, recurring, or increased purchase. Traditionally, brands stop their marketing and acquisition efforts at the moment of purchase, leading with a sales-minded point of view that results in poor customer satisfaction, defection, and increased advertising costs to reach and persuade the defected consumers to purchase again. As marketing mastermind Theodore Levitt said, "It's five times more expensive to create a customer than it is to keep a customer." Leading with a lifetime-value mindset, Experience Brands produce operational efficiency while increasing short-term and long-term value with their consumers.

To find new ways to engage with and interact with consumers following a purchase, Experience Brands track and define opportunities based on interaction and preference. Learning how the consumer is using or sharing the product or service can create preference-driven opportunities to re-engage and find new moments of value, continuously pushing the relationship beyond transaction and ownership, and closer to a membership approach.

To create these moments of interaction, Experience Brands expand the consumer journey far beyond the research, shop and buy moments, and into the post-purchase, onboarding, support and repurchase phases, expanding the product and service into the experience customers receive throughout this crucial part of the journey. This shows consumers that their relationship means more than a simple purchase, or a single transaction, and that they deserve more in their relationship with brands they purchase from. These moments are:

Post Purchase

The post-purchase opportunity lies in the immediate reaction from the brand once it's purchased. This could be an e-commerce purchase, signing a contract, or purchasing in a store. This moment gives your brand the ability to increase satisfaction, minimize any remorse, and establish a solid footing in the service area of the consumer journey.

Onboarding

If your brand, product, service, or experience requires instructions for use or consumption, or even if you just want to seize the moment to let the consumer dig deeper into your brand experience, the onboarding phase is an opportune moment to fulfill your Experience Brand promise. This phase is found shortly after post-purchase, where excitement may still be running strong and emotions are still raw enough to overcome any obstacles and delight consumers in a brand experience.

Customer Support

The next type of interaction is when and if your customer requires support in some manner. Whether the product or service malfunctioned or if they have a general query, consumers may reach out for support at any given time. Aligning your brand's support program with the Experience Brand strategy ensures, not only a consistent experience for the consumer, but the opportunity to truly fulfill and live up to the brand promise. Remember, each interaction with the consumer, whether started for a good or a bad reason, is an opportunity to add value authentically as an Experience Brand.

Loyalty and Rewards

Through repeat consumption and interaction, brands have the unique ability to continuously engage, learn from, and reward consumer relationships. Brands like Starbucks, Delta, or even your local coffee shop have the repetitive touch points to expand personalization at scale for increased loyalty and rewards along the way. Creating and tracking moments of consumption, interaction, or repetition gives Experience Brands the ability to increase moments of loyalty and reward certain consumer behaviors.

Advocacy and Deals

The ultimate goals of the Membership phase of the consumer journey are repurchase and advocacy—consumers telling their network about their experience and recommending toward a purchase. Experience Brands have these interactions innately built into their consumer journey, offering deals, social currency, or even street credibility as a differentiating value that your brand can intentionally create for your consumer.

Repurchase

Finally, if everything listed above goes right, you'll have the opportunity and ability to ask for and gain a repurchase from the consumer. Each interaction or non-interaction that adds value to your consumer and fulfills your Experience Brand process leads you closer toward a repurchase, and even an expanded purchase.

MEMBERSHIP OVER OWNERSHIP

Experience Brands have a fundamental perspective about their consumers; they are "members" of their brands, not just owners of their products. Innately the idea of membership over ownership has an increased responsibility and accountability for the brand. Not only does it have to succeed once, but it has to repeatedly succeed, learn, and grow with the relationship; Experience Brands understand individual challenges and feelings and, ultimately, co-create a future with their consumers. Having a membership mentality while crafting your Experience Brand changes your consumer journey mapping. It evolves your cadence of messaging and increases the reasons to believe and to connect. Approaching the post-purchase and support phase of your consumer journey with a "member" mentality transforms your brand beyond its walls and truly into an Experience Brand.

Membership Strategy

Not all brands, products, services and experiences innately lend themselves to the membership mindset. And this methodology may not work for all audience types. However, every brand strategy, if created correctly offers some ability to think this way. And the results, whether directly or indirectly will have an impact on the symbiotic brand and consumer relationship. Whether your CPG company can offer direct-to-consumer relationships, or you're a parts manufacturer that can add value in the market through innovative thought leadership, or you're a technology company that offers seamless experiences with your tech stack, your brand can establish a membership strategy for those folks you directly affect.

Brand Strategy Meets Consumer Opportunities

Membership is a natural extension of your Experience Brand strategy. Once you establish the way that your brand should interact, progress, and build relationships with your customers, you expand this strategy into white-space opportunities as they are discovered. And using the foundation and footing you've established with your Go to Market and Anytime, Anywhere Commerce strategies, you have a clear sense of who your consumers are, what they expect from you, why they do business with you, and what they value. These previous interactions and touch points have created a tremendous amount of data and insight giving you the knowledge of their journey and who they are as individuals.

Armed with this information, Experience Brands extend past the moment of purchase and into the membership life-cycle. Here, Experience Brands create and orchestrate more personalized messaging, services, and even rewards. These strategies and actions are meant to continue to add value to the relationship with consumers, even while they aren't necessarily in a purchase mindset. This is where the true value exchange happens for the consumer. By creating mechanisms to engage and re-engage owners as members, Experience Brands offer different types of value exchange for their customers.

- Rewards and Loyalty programs like Delta or American Express.
- Bespoke service offerings that can only be accessed if you're a member of the brand.
- Social currency, by giving members sharable discounts or offers to give to their networks.
- Co-Creation of products, services, or experiences to make their voices heard and establish relationships.

All of these value exchanges add a tremendous amount of value to the consumer relationship. They also create an opportunity for your brand to charge a premium or monetize the membership experience, even after purchase. This level of post-purchase service can become an extremely valuable opportunity for both the consumer and the Experience Brand.

OPERATIONALIZING MEMBERSHIP

Traditional companies are set up as marketing organizations to drive acquisition, and sales and service, to get to and through purchase. Rarely do the two meet and rarely are their strategies aligned to ensure a consistent experience for the consumer. Marketing, with the acquisition mindset is focused on getting new consumers in the funnel, while the sales and service departments are focused on getting as quickly as possible to a repurchase. Experience Brands look at this transition as an opportunity to learn, to continuously fulfill their brand promise, and to work toward creating new value for their consumers. They know the best experience they create will turn into loyalty and advocacy organically. This pushes the idea of marketing and relationship building through the entirety of the consumer journey.

This approach gives Experience Brands a new perspective on the consumers that purchase from them. They look through the lens of membership versus ownership. Membership takes the role of service far beyond a transaction and into the experience the consumer has with a brand. These moments don't just happen at moments of purchase, but in the little things and the personalization elements that treat the consumer like a valued member of the brand, not just someone who may happen to buy a product or service.

One thing that Experience Brands have found is the vast amount of opportunity to interact with and service consumers on an individual level post purchase, without the use of media or other marketing expenses. These moments—on-boarding, support, rewards, customer service, and repurchase—are ripe with opportunities to reaffirm the purchase decision, gain consumer feedback, thank customers for their business, reward their usage, and find new ways to ask for a repeat or expanded purchase. All are made easier by the personalized recommendations and engagement throughout the entire consumer journey.

Understanding the insights and learning from the consumer

experience across Go to Market, Commerce, and Membership gives Experience Brands what's needed to evolve their business models in ways that continually add value in the consumer marketplace.

www.JourneyEconomy.com/chapter-9

#membership@PaulMiser

LESSONS LEARNED

- The post-purchase time in the consumer journey is ripe with opportunity to continuously engage with consumers, finding new ways to add value, and capturing valuable data on the consumer, the product, and service. These actions will increase the probability of repeat purchase and provide insight to new revenue streams and business models.

- Expanding the consumer journey map to service and loyalty, Experience Brands intentionally create moments of exceptional service and rewards to reengage consumers and establish the brand promise through fulfillment.

- Experience Brands view the consumers who do make purchase as members in their brand's story—not just owners of a product or service. This mindset puts more responsibility and accountability on the brand to create more value throughout the entirety of the relationship.

CHAPTER 10

BUSINESS MODEL

NEW WAYS TO CREATE REVENUE
WHILE ADDING VALUE

"A business model describes how your company creates, delivers and captures value."

Steve Blank

WHEN helping Lincoln transform its brand from an Auto Manufacturer to a luxury mobility provider, we took an approach to look at the entirety of the situation at hand. We looked at consumer trends, business needs, mobility trends, and technology advances—all to get a sense of where we were and where things are going. With that information, we expanded the North Star brand strategy to support the evolution of the brand and of the value that the brand will ultimately provide for the consumer and within the personal transportation industry. We found that the way to make money wasn't necessarily by selling more cars. The biggest challenge was that we didn't really have a baseline or idea of what revenue would supplement or augment the growth of the brand and of the business. So, we expanded our trend analysis into business model trends in and around the personal transportation industry as well as other industries to start to build some testable hypotheses.

We found some short-term and longer-term opportunities to conceptualize, prototype, and test. Then we created pilots to test, using existing assets, elements, and relationships at our disposal to bring to market. These included mobility services like parking and car sharing; to service oriented offerings like Pickup and Delivery for service and maintenance; to rewards programs that consumers would subscribe to. Each pilot proved successful in its own right and allowed us to gain valuable in-market consumer data. It also allowed us to understand and plan which business models would prove to be effective in generating revenue at scale. The programs that added symbiotic value to the brand-consumer relationship stayed; the others were either put on a roadmap, pivoted, or killed. This process and approach are really what this chapter is all about—evolving the business model.

The last play in the Growth Action Plan is the expansion and evolution of everything before it—from Go to Market, to Commerce, to Membership. It is focused on leveraging insight, data and trends to create new value and revenue through the business model. Technological and consumer behaviors have forever changed the way companies can build revenue streams. Experience Brands have embraced these trends for the continued success of their consumer value proposition and, in turn, their revenue. By packaging their products, services, and experiences in new ways, Experience Brands have started to lean into new revenue streams through new offerings, redefined value propositions, or recurring revenue. All of these revenue generating opportunities are found and intentionally built throughout the entire consumer experience, which is becoming a treasure trove of value.

In fact, according to Forrester Research, for every point increase in Consumer Experience score, companies can expect:

- Retailers – $244 Million Incremental Revenue
- Banks – $123 Million Incremental Revenue
- Airlines – $167 Million Incremental Revenue
- Health Insurers – 150,000 New Customers
- Hotels – $330 Million Incremental Revenue

DIGITAL BUSINESS MODELS

Activating a new business model can be additive, innovative, or cannibalistic to the core business. Experience Brands understand the pros and cons and test against hypotheses in order to find the best business model for today and tomorrow, letting old models fade away to support the future growth of the brand. As we see below, technology has provided new ways to generate revenue. Experience Brands use these models as standalone, combined with each other, or integrated into traditional models to support their brand's experience strategy. There is no right or wrong business model, only ones that are right or wrong for your Experience Brand strategy.

E-Commerce / Marketplace

This allows users to buy from a website or their mobile devices directly from a manufacturer, retailer, or a reseller. Examples of this are Zappos, Amazon, and Alibaba.

On-Demand

This model has users pay for a service they don't have time to do for themselves, allowing someone else to do it for them. Examples of this are Uber, Lyft, or Home Advisor.

Subscription

Usually a monthly or annual fee for continued access to a product or service. Examples are Netflix, Hulu, or Salesforce.

Freemium

This includes either offering a free trial or a free level of service (usually ad-supported) providing value to upsell into a premium or paid model. Examples of this are Spotify, Dropbox, or Mailchimp.

Hidden Revenue

Here users gain access to a product or service with the revenue happening behind the scenes between the platform and another third party. Examples of this are Facebook and Google.

Peer-To-Peer

This model is based on the mindset of access over ownership. Here the user pays for access or usage of a product or service over owning it. Examples of this are Uber, Airbnb, or LinkedIn.

Ad-Supported

In exchange for free service or content, a user will be exposed to advertising, usually targeted by demographic, psychographic, and behavior data. Examples of this are Google, Quora, or New York Times.

Open Source

This model provides free software that can be edited by a community. These businesses usually provide upgrades to premium features. Examples of this are Redhat or Github.

REVENUE MODEL CREATION

Revenue follows perceived value from a consumer. This revenue creation can take on many different shapes. From increased revenue through charging a premium for an enhanced experience, to net new revenue opportunities through new markets or products, to different revenue models by packaging up and deploying your current offerings in a new way.

Opportunity identification

Leveraging insight across the consumer journey and throughout the elements of this Growth Action Plan, Experience Brands are continuously looking for the pain points to create new value for their customers, thus new value for their brand. Using data like journey drop off rates, customer satisfaction scores, pricing models, or even defection rates, Experience Brands can identify further pain points to remove, or trends in consumer behavior on which to capitalize.

Value Creation

Once they understand the ongoing opportunities, Experience Brands create a symbiotic value between consumer and brand, finding a new offering while also finding new revenue opportunities. This value creation is a combination of products, services, and business models, giving consumers something new, something easier, or something exciting.

Revenue Modeling

Technology changes how and where we can transact, but it also changes the measurement of product usage and recurrence of transaction, opening the aperture of revenue models. Many Experience Brands are looking for ways to create recurring revenue models. However, there are many ways

Experience Brands are building revenue using digital business models.

When planning for strategic growth, companies are faced with an obvious challenge: Are we providing the right value for consumers in the marketplace? The answer most of the time is really a non-answer: "We have a product or service that we advertise in order to drive revenue and profits." This mindset is rooted in the paralysis of "we've always done it this way."

However, consumers and industries are quickly waking up to the economic reality that value propositions are shifting as is revenue along with those preferences and decisions—rendering the growth strategy of advertising alone ineffective or only marginally useful.

Shifting consumer expectations and value propositions are driven primarily through the business model within the consumer experience. Growth leaders and disruptors are identifying and deploying new strategies that continuously enhance the symbiotic value exchange between brand and consumer. However, they are not creating new products and services, but looking at serving their customers in new ways.

Benedict Evans, a startup founder and industry analyst, recently published a presentation, *Tech in 2020: Standing on the Shoulders of Giants*, where he discusses how technology is driving business and consumer behavior. He provides a great overview on how things are evolving and the economic viewpoint of what is next.

The way that these Experience Brands are finding and creating growth in their business model is looking at their value proposition in four new ways:

- Vertical Integration
- Horizontal Expansion
- Unbundling
- Bundling

VERTICAL/HORIZANTAL INTEGRATION

Vertical Integration

Vertical integration adds value to the top or bottom of your organization based on the current offering or industry your company is in. Here, the value is created by network effects in the development of an ecosystem.

For example, quip, the electric toothbrush startup, has started to create an ecosystem of oral health. They have expanded their offerings beyond the toothbrush and into other products like toothpaste, floss, etc. The interesting thing is they have also purchased a dental insurance company and started to partner with dental practices to provide more, connected value to their consumers around their oral health.

Ford launched FordPass a few years ago as their foray into mobility. FordPass offers access beyond the physical relationship with the product (controlling the vehicle), but has integrated to other aspects of driving or transportation. The program connects to enhanced dealer services, provides access to parking and refueling, and has a loyalty program built in to reward driver behavior. This seems to be building

the foundation of an ecosystem of mobility that will help the organization usher in a future of autonomous driving.

Horizontal Expansion

Horizontal expansion adds value by expanding your organization in new service areas through new products and services in adjacent or tertiary industries or marketplaces. Here, value is created through a flywheel of value that can quickly expand into new markets with new service or product offerings.

All of the trillion-dollar companies (Alphabet, Amazon, Apple, Microsoft) are experts at this. They have built massive amounts of value by leveraging their position in their core markets to flywheel out to other services and offerings. Whether it is expanding into the cloud like Azure or AWS, or getting into voice like Alexa or Siri, or integrating with physical hardware like Fire or Surface, these organizations are continuously finding and creating value horizontally by adding new service and product offerings in new markets.

UNBUNDLING/BUNDLING

Unbundling

Unbundling, as we're seeing in many industries like entertainment, automotive, and retail, is the act of removing options or elements of the business offering to return to the essence of the value exchange. Here, value is created through "disruption" by effectively unbundling complex business organizations and stripping them down to a core element. Consumers have been shifting their behaviors and decisions to companies that offer simplicity in process and value.

For example, Netflix has disrupted the media and entertainment industry by unbundling cable offerings and providing users with direct access to content on one portal. They've expanded this service by creating custom programming, but all through one personalized portal versus a package of channels.

Uber shifted the taxi and limousine industry by unbundling the process of access to transportation. They targeted the pain point of dispatching and waiting for a taxi by connecting the driver directly with the rider—forever transforming the industry.

Casper has started to transform the consumer behaviors in the mattress marketplace by unbundling the process of shopping for and buying a mattress. They targeted the pain point of going into a physical store, by providing a direct-to-consumer solution through e-commerce.

Bundling

Bundling, on the other hand is the act of adding new offerings to an already effective value proposition. Here, value is created by bundling products, services, and, now, experiences together. While this isn't a new practice, the way it is manifesting in the Journey Economy is. NYU Professor and Marketing pundit Scott Galloway has coined the term "rundle," which is the idea of bundling products and services into a subscription-type model to create recurring revenue for organizations.

Examples of bundling are:

Apple, at its core, is a device or hardware manufacturer. However, with the connectivity of their devices and scale of their market penetration, they have been able to release new products and services that add value to the consumer and their bottom line. With services like Music, Arcade, TV+ and News, Apple has created massive present value as well as future value for their organization.

Nike has started to jump on this trend as well. Nike has started to create experiences like Nike Training Club which bundles product and content in a way that fulfills its brand promise. They also recently launched Nike Adventure Club. This is a subscription model for parents to have access to new shoes for their kids on an as-needed basis.

The act of bundling or unbundling adds or removes products and services from your organizational offering. These actions are done in two ways across the organization, vertically or horizontally.

• • •

EXPERIENCE BRAND PROFILE: APPLE
Expanding from Core, to Service, to Experience

As the reigning Trillion-Dollar Champ, Apple has made some smart decisions over the last few years to capitalize on the transformation toward becoming an Experience Brand. We have to remember: the core of Apple's business is the devices they manufacture. However, the connectivity and usage of these devices has opened a tremendous amount of opportunity to build new revenue streams for the business. As these evolve, the core business starts to shift into an experience-driven organization—increasing the value of the consumer relationship as well as the company. As you can see below, Apple expanded vertically through device manufacturing while expanding horizontally with incremental value in what their products can create. The next step would be to create bundles of their services to support a longer-term, more-personalized relationship.

Apple Devices

The core business drivers include Mac, iPhone, iWatch, iPad and others. These become the entry point into the evolution of the brand value.

Apple Music

Building on iTunes and Beats Music, Apple Music is a music subscription service that competes with Spotify and Pandora.

Apple News

Apple News is an aggregator of news and publisher content, based on personal preferences. There is a free version built into its devices, but also a subscription model that gets through paywalls of some publishers.

Apple Arcade

Much like Apple Music and Apple News, Apple wants to capitalize on the trends of gaming across device. It is a subscription service for access to specific game titles.

Apple TV+

Building on Apple TV over the last few years, Apple leveraged consumer data and consumption trends to provide access to original and third-party content, competing with Netflix and Hulu.

Apple Pay and Apple Card

To capitalize on the trends of contactless payment and omni-channel commerce, Apple has launched Apple Pay and Apple Card to get into financial services.

• • •

EXPERIENCE BRAND PROFILE: NIKE
Living the Brand Value Through Membership and Subscription

Expanding on the transformation Nike is making in the Omni-channel Commerce environment, it has started to change its business model to support the core business. Not only has it launched several lifestyle apps and initiatives (e.g. Nike FuelBand, Nike Run Club) to gather consumer data, but it has also started to try different types of subscription models. It fulfills its brand promise, "if you have a body, you're an athlete," by providing the tools, content, and product for different consumer types.

Nike Training Club

The Nike Training Club App is geared toward capitalizing on the at-home fitness trend fueled by Peloton, Mirror, and others. The app is a monthly subscription fee providing access to over 185 different workouts along with access to tools to support personal training and goals.

Nike Adventure Club

Nike Adventure Club is a subscription model for parents to remove the worry of shopping for shoes as their kids outgrow them. For a monthly fee, users can select how many pairs of shoes per year they'd want to receive. The shoes are paired with personalized activities to support active lifestyles.

CREATING VALUE TO BUILD REVENUE

Opportunity abounds throughout the consumer journey. Using the consumer journey as a map, our Experience Brand strategy as our compass, and technology as our ship, we can chart a new course for our business model. Finding and identifying consumer pain points and white-space opportunities through consumer feedback, Experience Brands are creating new business models to capture consumer behaviors and expectations which they use to transform their industries. Experience Brands use these digital business models to change the value they offer to their consumers.

www.JourneyEconomy.com/chapter-10

#businessmodel@PaulMiser

LESSONS LEARNED

- By intimately knowing, tracking, and refining the consumer journey, Experience Brands have the unique ability to identify the pain points consumers have when shopping for, buying, and owning a product or service in their category. By removing these pain points, Experience Brands create immediate value that can result in operational efficiency, and also new revenue.

- Technology advancements have changed the essence of traditional business models. By leveraging the business model trends created by technology, Experience Brands can establish new relationships with their customers, resulting in new value and revenue.

- These new experiences and business models give Experience Brands the ability to charge a premium on their traditional products and services, but they also can find new ways to make or generate revenue.
- Experience Brands create new revenue in many different ways, but most fall within four shifts: expanding horizontally or moving vertically; unbundling complex business models or bundling products, services and experiences to create new value for the revenue exchange.

IMPLEMENTATION

"The greatest danger in times of turbulence is not the turbulence
—it is to act with yesterday's logic."

Peter Drucker

CHAPTER 11

OPERATIONALIZATION

GETTING TO ORGANIZATIONAL ACCEPTANCE

"In the end, strategy is nothing but good intentions unless it's effectively implemented."

Clayton Christensen

WORKING with and within both large, complex Fortune 500 organizations and startups alike, I'm always amazed at the energy it takes to make change. Whether it's a re-org or a complete digital transformation, there are always challenges and barriers that require planning, communication, consensus, ownership, accountability, transparency, and most of all purpose. Without these elements, there will never be organizational acceptance of the strategy that is being implemented as it will always be something that is forced on the enterprise, not embraced. Experience Brands have become masters of change by becoming masters of agility. One of their superpowers is the ability to move faster in the marketplace than their traditional counterparts. This characteristic is a competitive advantage allowing them to identify and act on opportunities more quickly than other companies in the market. And in today's Journey Economy, this could mean the difference between growth or failure.

Operationalizing your Experience Brand strategy creates clarity in a world of uncertainty. The power is in implementation. As we saw coming into 2020, having a strategy is crucial to understanding the path your brand is taking. However, it must include the agility to pivot, pause, or scale as the market fluctuates. Implementing an Experience Brand strategy in the Journey Economy is extremely similar. To maximize success and effectiveness, the operationalization of the strategy should be implemented across the organization in a phased rollout, giving your brand the ability to test, learn, and optimize along the way. Working in this manner creates an always-on, evolving mindset versus the stop-start process of traditional organizations.

There is no better example than having watched Experience Brands navigate the COVID-19 Pandemic in 2020. They capitalized on operationalizing the core elements of their organizations to satisfy and fulfill their Experience Brand strategies at scale. Having their North Star defined, and their consumer journey mapped, they were able to find and capitalize on opportunities by leveraging the shifting marketplace to max-imize value for their consumers. This success wasn't happen-stance, but rather a meticulous creation of an organization and enterprise to have the ability to move quickly and pivot when needed, all while maintaining their brand promise ful-fillment and symbiotic value exchanges with their consumers.

Part 4 is broken into three phases of ongoing implementation of the Experience Brand strategy:

Chapter 11 is focused on the foundational elements of cre-ating an organization ready and willing to change.

Chapter 12 illustrates the process to implement change.

Chapter 13 outlines the approach to measure, optimize and evolve the strategic change on an ongoing basis, continu-ously adding value to the consumer relationship.

These crucial phases will give your organization the insight and ability to see around corners when implementing your Experience Brand strategy. They will also provide you clarity on common pitfalls along the way. The investment made in implementation of your Experience Brand strategy will deliver results in the short-term but will substantially increase the likelihood of step-change success in the long-term.

CORE ELEMENTS OF OPERATIONALIZATION

There are four core elements for preparing your organization for the operationalization of your Experience Brand strategy. Each element is focused on providing clarity, giving you the tools for successful implementation, and ultimately, clearing the path toward execution.

Strategic Roadmap

Doing the consumer journey map and Experience Brand strategy work gives you both a North Star of where your brand is going as well as a list of initiatives to tackle to bring your brand toward that North Star in the form of a strategic roadmap. The strategic roadmap is rooted in solving challenges for your consumer, whether removing pain points and chores or maximizing moments of joy. Each initiative on the roadmap should bring you a step closer toward becoming an Experience Brand while bringing you one step closer to your consumer. As seen in the Delta example, you need an all-of-organization approach from a top-down vision to working-level action. The clear point of view about where the organization is heading with a clear sense of how to get there, gives Experience Brands like Delta the ability to move quickly and gain organization-wide consensus.

Dynamic Prioritization

This strategic roadmap is a prioritized list of initiatives and charters that your organization must execute to become an Experience Brand. The roadmap is a living and breathing artifact that becomes dynamic as the market or consumer behaviors shift. However, the prioritization must be established on the Experience Brand principles established in the Experience Brand strategy development, and not on any internal bureaucracy. The key to the roadmap and its prioritization is to continuously maximize and add new value to your customers throughout their journey and relationship with your brand.

Return on Investment (ROI)

One crucial element of the prioritization of the strategic roadmap that will aid in consensus, ownership, and accountability, is the Return on Investment the initiatives brings the organization. The ROI of the strategic roadmap is a simple one—does the initiative add more value to the symbiotic relationship when implemented? From a business standpoint, this value could be reduced operating costs, efficiency in organizational restructuring, increased revenue opportunities, or, the holy grail, net new revenue opportunities. However, consumers are looking at ROR or the Return on Relationship with your brand. These would include saving time, saving money, feeling understood and a sense of belonging, having a sense of novelty, or just help with solving problems in a unique way.

Action Plan

Having a clear Experience Brand strategy and focused strategic roadmap provides clarity of purpose, action, and transparency. Understanding the value of the initiatives and the role each person plays in that value gives ownership to those implementing the initiative while communicating to the rest of the organization how it fits into the bigger picture. This action plan gives employees and even consumers a sense of what's to come so they can be invested in the journey as it unfolds.

Talent: Future of Work

Whether it's been scaling or reorganizing the workforce, Experience Brands have been able to maximize the current and immediate future state of their brand vision with their consumer by redefining the future of work for the brand and its talent. One of the biggest transformations of the Journey Economy has been the disruption and restructuring of human capital across most industries. We've witnessed historic levels of layoffs and unemployment, while at the same time experiencing increased need for an essential and supply-chain workforce. The role that human capital plays in your Experience Brand strategy will change and evolve as well, giving you the ability to navigate through and pivot around market shifts as they arise.

There has never been a workforce opportunity like we're seeing right now. With the vast amount of talent readily available paired with accelerated downsized businesses, we can take this time to rethink the future of work for our brands. What talent do we need to fulfill our Experience Brand strategy? What does our workflow look like? What about our offices? How can technology support our human capital to make them more connected and more effective?

As we're implementing our Experience Brand strategy, we are being forced to break down internal organizational silos to support a consumer-centric experience. Having this holistic view of the consumers and their journey, we can then model our organization to best respond to this transformation. Starting with understanding the best structure for the response, the specific talent we need, and the technology needed to empower them.

Restructuring

Becoming more consumer-centric to deliver an Experience Brand strategy, your organizations needs to break down silos and create a holistic view of consumers and their journey. Taking this time to restructure is crucial for short-term success and long-term scale.

Reskill or Upskill

There is a talent pool like never before. There are skills needed that we've never had before. Rebuilding your organization will be a combination of finding new talent and reskilling or upskilling existing talent, making your organization more agile and readily available to pivot if and when necessary.

Human + Technology

Technology is the great enabler of strategy. Pairing the right tech stack with human capital expands effectiveness, efficiency, and what's possible for the consumer experience.

Process: Agility

With a foundational understanding of the North Star strategy along with the consumer journey defined, Experience Brands have been able to pivot quickly to respond to consumer needs and behaviors through process. Building a process that scales and evolves with the consumer and the situation is a key factor of the success of any consumer experience or Experience Brand strategy. Having a holistic view of the consumer journey along with your brand's response creates the need for a massive orchestration of elements, capital, and assets to support consumer needs and expectations. This orchestration is crucial for maximizing the value exchange between your consumer and your brand.

The orchestration of the process needs to remove the pain points of the consumer and the employees executing the strategy to become as efficient as possible. The process also needs to be aware of the moments where the brand promise becomes fulfilled. Doing so connects the dots between marketing, the supply chain, and the eventual consumption of your brand's product or service.

Marketing and Relationship

Leveraging the consumer journey and the Experience Brand strategy, your brand will create an always-on marketing and relationship-building approach. These relationships are created through interaction, fueled by data, and personalized through retention.

Supply Chain

Marketing and Relationship expands beyond mere advertising and content development. There is transparency and expectation found throughout the entire supply chain in how the product is developed or how the service is rendered.

Transaction / Logistics / Consumption

The culmination of everything in the process is the moment of transaction, expectation, or consumption created by the consumer's purchase decision. Having these moments fulfill the brand promise is crucial to your Experience Brand strategy because it creates or diminishes value more than any other element in the process.

Technology: Connected Experiences

With the acceleration of consumer behaviors in the Journey Economy, there's no doubt about the role technology plays in creating the holistic journey for the consumer experience. Connecting marketing to the supply chain to logistics creates a singular experience for these transformed behaviors and expectations. Technology enables your Experience Brand strategy, not the other way around. As we're witnessing with the successful Experience Brands in today's Journey Economy, technology is the power that runs their experience and business model. An Experience Brand technology approach is created by three different stacks.

Brand Stack

The Brand Stack is the technology that powers the front end of the brand relationship. It's the CRM, data and algorithms that make the decisions for the Experience Brand strategy. The Brand Stack is modeled after the consumer journey maps.

Experience Stack

The Experience Stack is the technology that enables the interaction and value exchange between consumer and brand. This includes all AdTech and Martech solutions as well as websites, e-commerce, chat bots, etc. The Experience Stack effectively generates the experience for the consumer.

Enterprise Stack

The Enterprise Stack is the underlying technology that connects the Brand and Experience Stacks with the enterprise of the business. This includes the supply chain, transaction information, connected products, and cross-channel data. This layer provides the analytics and insights across all stacks to make business decisions to pivot, pause, or scale.

CHALLENGES FACING IMPLEMENTATION

By coordinating the people, processes, and technology of your organization to support the development and implementation of your Experience Brand strategy, you're setting the foundation for true change management and scale. Having the right people, creating new connected-processes, and deploying the right technology are the three ingredients Experience Brands have in their recipe for success. However, there will be challenges, roadblocks, and barriers to overcome. Change is never easy but understanding the common pitfalls will give you the knowledge to power through and continue on.

Clarity in Strategy

The biggest challenge Experience Brand leaders face is clarity of strategy. It's easy to get bogged down in the details of process or technology, but without the proper Experience Brand strategy, this change by itself becomes a moot point.

The reason for this transformation is to open new opportunities for the enterprise to succeed, both internally and externally, in the short-term and the long-term alike. True transformation happens when a business rallies behind a succinct and focused strategy, letting technology enable the elements of that strategy in coming to life.

Skills

For some elements of the Experience Brand strategy, there is a skills shortage in today's marketplace. This is why Experience Brands are dedicated to creating, up-skilling, or cross-skilling initiatives to better empower their workforce with the expertise and talent needed to move to the next level. However, the skills shortage doesn't have to hinder the strategic development of Experience Transformation. For too long, organizations have put different departments like IT, Marketing, Sales and Service, and Product in their own work streams, hoping there will be an innate integration in approach, which is rarely the case. To kickstart the transformation to Experience Brand, business leaders are bringing these roles and departments together to aid in the strategy development and implementation planning. Having all business voices at the table is just as important as the voice of the customer or corporate development. They go hand in hand.

Reluctance to Embrace Change

Any kind of change in an organization creates employee reluctance, which is why it is crucial that Experience Brand strategies have an operationalization plan that delivers new working processes, procedures, and protocols. Successful Experience Brands have a "top down, bottom up" approach to transformation implementation. This is where there is a consistent cadence of focused communication from the Executive Leadership about the what, why, and how of the transformation and a manager-level implementation plan that brings the workforce along with the work-habit changes.

Legacy

Many organizations are faced with managing the status quo of business today while preparing for the future. In larger organizations, the status quo of the short-term business results usually has a louder voice than the long-term planning. So, there is definitely a reluctance to upset the mission-critical systems that keep the organization running. This mindset is one rooted in legacy—legacy thinking, processes, technologies, and structure. The process to overcome legacy issues, is to use a phased approach for implementation, gaining small wins along the way, making incremental gains to build momentum. Some Experience Brands also use the approach of parallel implementation, where the Experience Brand initiatives are implemented in parallel to the status quo, legacy systems. This coordinated approach follows the same change management methodology but implemented differently.

Silos

Silos are probably the biggest obstacle facing the Experience Brand transformation. Usually, business units within an organization were established to solve for a specific action, like marketing or sales, or service or support. These functions may be discreet within the organization, but for the consumer they are viewed as one company. Syncing these units and activities together for a singular relationship with the consumer is the real impetus for Experience Brand transformation. This is where the overarching business strategy comes into play. Having a singular focus for the organization with a shared set of incentives, gives business units a playbook that fits into the broader vision, versus a separate goal as before.

Leadership Skills

The Experience Brand business leaders that are emerging and proving successful in the Journey Economy often come from a technology-driven background versus the manufacturing-minded leaders of the past. The underlying view of business may remain the same; however, the skills needed to succeed as an Experience Brand have evolved. The biggest skill that I've seen emerge is agility. Business leaders of today are performing in a fast-paced, continuously changing world where new technologies and disruptors are continuously changing consumer behaviors and the value propositions they expect. This puts a lot of strain on business planning and the executive leadership in the organization. Agility becomes the single most important skill business leaders need to succeed with digital transformation and in today's business environment as a whole. I believe that agility is made up of the soft skills of curiosity, optimism, systems-thinking, and grit. It takes this combination of openness and rigor to have the ability to take risks and identify new ideas while staying the course of the broader business strategy.

THE FOUNDATION FOR CHANGE IS SET

Preparing for change is as important as executing the change. Aligning the vision and strategy for your Experience Brand transformation with the people, processes, and technologies needed to execute, you prepare the foundational elements of the organization for change. Leveraging these core resources and organizational assets, your organization will be able to begin implementing your Strategic Roadmap through a rigorous change-management approach geared to gain consensus, garner transparency and accountability, and build momentum for full transformation, optimization, and evolution.

Experience Brand transformation isn't just updating technology systems, rather it is an opportunity to reframe and overhaul the entire business value proposition, from finding efficiency in processes and operations to building new products, services, experiences, and business models for consumer value. Today's business leaders look at this transformation as strategic business planning that uses technology to expand their business's potential. Therefore, this transformation isn't something to be done in a silo but should be viewed as an integrated process to prepare the enterprise for continuous value creation for the future.

www.JourneyEconomy.com/chapter-11

#operationalization@PaulMiser

LESSONS LEARNED

- Your operationalization strategy and approach are just as important as your Experience Brand strategy. Not only does the organization have to align on a common vision and strategy but the whole of the organization needs to rally and transform to support it.

- Your talent will become the lifeblood of the success of your Experience Brand. The skill sets, the collaborative environment, and the technology support will give your people the purpose and the ability to thrive in the orchestration of your Experience Brand.
- Stripping away the mindset of "this is how we've always done it" will give your brand the ability to transform its business processes for the benefit of the consumer experience. By connecting business units and consumers correctly, your Experience Brand strategy will be set up for success.
- Technology is the enabler to great success. Experience Brands can only go as far as their systems and technologies will allow. Creating the right tech stack to fulfill your Experience Brand strategy is crucial to its ongoing implementation and evolution.
- There are challenges with all important things. Understanding and overcoming these challenges give Experience Brands a clearer focus and strategy to succeed.

CHAPTER 12

CHANGE MANAGEMENT

BRINGING YOUR EXPERIENCE BRAND TO SCALE

"Change before you have to."
Jack Welch

I HAVE spent my career creating, launching and scaling digital business units for large organizations, so I've had the opportunity to learn, firsthand, what change management looks like. Each and every project or initiative was a change for the organization, using muscles they've never used before and pulling levers they never thought possible. Change of this nature can seem daunting when looking at it from a holistic perspective. But if there is one thing I've learned along the way, change happens over time. It's rarely a singular moment where the past was the past and the future is now. Change has always been a concerted, focused effort to systematically implement structures, processes and technologies executed by a cross-functional team of change agents.

Throughout the course of this chapter, we'll dive deeper into how to actually manage the change. This requires looking at methodologies rooted in agility, transparency in communication—how and what to communicate—the mechanics of change management, and tools that help document and guide the journey. Once established, this approach to change management can become the operating system for your organization for ongoing measurement, optimization, and evolution for your Experience Brand.

METHODOLOGY

To start the journey of your organization's Experience Brand transformation, we need to set a few ground rules and perspectives. The way that Experience Brand organizations approach change management are completely different than those at more established, traditional organizations. This perspective allows them to not only move quickly and pivot, but also to build strong relationships with their consumers along the way. This perspective is crucial for success and for the evolution of your Experience Brand.

Lean Startup Methodology

The Lean Startup Methodology popularized by Eric Reis is an approach to agile software development to create quick product-market fit by launching a minimum viable product into the marketplace to gather quick consumer feedback. This feedback is then used to optimize the product for the audience need. Then launch, learn, and optimize again. This methodology has become the standard of operation for the startup culture, and it has taken hold in larger enterprises as well. In his follow up book, *The Startup Way*, Reis brings the methodology to these more traditional organizations.

Throughout the course of my career and the change management I've led, I've leaned heavily on this methodology to ensure we are making progress while learning as much as we can along the way. This methodology, if used correctly, will help your organization implement your Experience Brand strategy. After all, the root of the Experience Brand strategy is to continuously add value for consumers by intentionally creating the consumer journey they take to do business with your brand. Doing this with an incremental, iterative approach gives you the feedback and insight needed to ensure you're solving this challenge. You are not just guessing and building in the background, only to launch and miss the mark. Relationships are iterative. Experiences are iterative. This methodology gives you that power.

The basics of the Lean Startup Methodology add texture and construct to your strategic roadmap. By looking at the initiatives you have decided to tackle you can leverage this methodology to begin executing now.

Minimum Viable Product (MVP): An MVP is the starting point for a solution to use to gather feedback in the marketplace. It's never used as an end solution. If it has too many features, functions, bells or whistles, the core value you're providing may be lost in complexity. The MVP is the very essence of solving the problem. This will evolve and iterate over time but will do so with real interaction and feedback from your consumer and other stakeholders.

The process that Reis established in his book is:

Ideas → Build → Product → Measure → Data → Learn

Actionable Metrics: Creating a testing curriculum for each initiative gives you a hypothesis in how the MVP or iteration will perform in the market as well as the metrics that you will measure against to prove the release is solving the problem correctly. These metrics should be actionable to take back into development and execution.

Testing: Testing can take on many different forms. You might have qualitative insights directly from the consumer or quantitative measures from passive actions with the product, service, or experience. Many problems that we're trying to solve can have multiple solutions. To ensure you are solving them in a way that fulfills your Experience Brand strategy, you can establish A/B split tests to test multiple solutions against the testing criteria.

Pivot: With the feedback and results from the testing, you will have the insight available to iterate on the solution. With this methodology, failing fast is a good thing. If your solution misses the mark, you have the insight and knowledge to make a pivot toward a stronger solution. This is where the power in the process comes into play. By building the ability to make fast pivots like this, you are opening a new world for your business and Experience Brand strategy.

Evolving the Strategic Roadmap

By evolving the roadmap or strategic plan to parse out each initiative into MVPs and a testing curriculum, you gain a sense of control for execution and management. Each initiative should have concept, test, launch, pivot, and scale decisions created to ensure you are moving forward and delivering quick progress and results for your business. The results, whether positive, negative, pivot, or scale, can be contextualized as opportunities to communicate across the organization. These moments of decision and optimization aid in organizational acceptance and buy-in. Over time, you will start to generate the momentum needed to make bigger change transformations as your strategic roadmap requires.

COMMUNICATION

The next crucial aspect for change management is communication. Communication is key anytime you're doing something different in an organization. In fact, erring on the side of over-communication is probably good advice. Not only do you maintain transparency and accountability, but you also provide knowledge, insights, and opportunities for ways the organization can become more valuable to your customers. But the question becomes what to communicate and how to communicate it. "What" to communicate is broken down two ways:

What are we doing and why? (The Process)
How is it working? (The Outcomes)

How to communicate will be covered in the change management section later in the chapter.

The Process

Vision and Brand Promise: To quote Steven Covey, "We must seek first to understand, then to be understood." Truly understanding your consumer's needs and how your company and products can fulfill those needs is critical to any type of business, but especially necessary when building a digitally powered business. This understanding not only gives us the insight to communicate what our brands and products are all about, but also allows us to see how the brand promise will be fulfilled across each consumer's journey.

Experience Brand Strategy: Once we have an understanding of who we are, what we stand for, and how we'll fulfill the brand promise to our consumer, we can build a strategy that effectively supports and activates the brand. This includes messaging, interaction models, transactions, service, design, and even the essence of business models to some extent. Anything that drives your business or consumer relationship should communicate or fulfill your brand and product promise.

Current State (Consumer Journey): Now let's get into the weeds a bit. If you're an established organization, you have a consumer journey currently. It might not be the best, but at least you can map the current state to get a benchmark of what you are working with. This audit should include everything from technology systems, service design, marketing, operations, and supply chain and should be mapped across the consumer journey from unaware through to repurchase and advocacy.

Future State (Consumer Journey):   Let's get out of the weeds and into the clouds. Starting with a fresh sheet of paper or whiteboard, what would the ideal consumer journey look like using your brand promise and strategy. Work as though you are starting your business over with no legacy issues translating into the future. Start from initial awareness through to advocacy for your product. Focus on the consumer needs, not the organizational needs. Find ways to truly fulfill your brand promise and understand which transactions and interactions will do that best for your customers. Map all of this out and identify which technologies, data, and platforms might support the activation of this dream state.

Gap Analysis and Strategic Roadmap: Now we mash the weeds with the clouds. Where are there gaps between the two worlds? This becomes your Strategic Roadmap. This exercise allows you to see where you're going, but it also gives you the insight to prioritize the technologies, user experience needs, and incremental products that can play a role in optimizing your organization. The thing to look at here isn't the whole, but the parts that you can start to take action on. Digital Transformation doesn't happen overnight. It's a continuous effort to go from today to tomorrow in a better, more efficient, and more engaging way for your consumer.

Design/Build/Test/Learn: Once you have your prioritized actions to build a better tomorrow, you can take a cue from Eric Reis and integrate some Lean Startup methodologies to get started on the continuous, evolutionary loop of Design/ Build/Test/Learn. This will not only give you the momentum to start taking action but also the flexibility to pivot and grow in response to consumers and their changing behaviors.

The Outcomes

There have been many case studies documenting how digital has completely changed an organization. Depending on your vision and strategy, you'll experience varying degrees of success, but if you stick to your essence as a brand and continuously strive to fulfill that promise at each touch point, you're likely to have great success as well.

Efficiency: By understanding how consumers, supply chains, and data flow, your organization can reap tremendous rewards from becoming more efficient. How much could your organization save if you could retain customers better, turn around an aircraft faster, reduce a step-in logistics, etc.?

Effectiveness and Revenue: Understanding your consumer and revenue model in a detailed way will help you become more effective in how you communicate and attract new consumers; you may also discover opportunities for incremental revenue.

Consumer Connection: Consumers are loyal and advocate for businesses that they truly trust and connect with. There is a reason why Amazon is one of the most loved companies in the world. They understand their consumers better than anyone else and they use that knowledge to continually add incremental value.

Funding/Incremental Revenue: A great misnomer in Digital Transformation is that it is a huge investment upfront without guaranteed success. Fortunately, that is a large myth that should be dispelled. The great thing about working in an evolutionary and iterative mindset, is that cost savings and incremental revenue can happen relatively quickly, providing your organization the savings or profit to continually reinvest in your digital transformation process.

Culture: I've heard many times from some of the largest companies in the world that "we want to act like a startup." They see the culture and excitement a startup has to offer and want to be a part of that magic and secret sauce. By preparing your organization for Digital Transformation, the culture will shift toward this mindset.

Digital Transformation isn't necessarily the cure for all that ails an organization, but the process is a great framework to identify those ailments and devise a solution around them. We are at a great moment in time where we can recreate our businesses for the future. Even if your organization has been around for hundreds of years, you have the power to take a step back, get back to your roots, and define what that means in this digital future we are in. It is a moment of empowerment and excitement and should never be seen as a moment of turmoil or anxiety.

CHANGE MANAGEMENT

Putting everything in this chapter together, we start our journey toward change management. By breaking down the strategic roadmap into smaller MVPs, putting a testing curriculum to them, iterating on them with results, and communicating that across the organization, you can gain quick ownership and understanding of what is happening. The path to becoming an Experience Brand will be a rewarding one, but will require collaboration, ownership, and momentum.

Framework

Change Management can take on many different forms within an organization. Working under an agreed upon established framework will give your organization the consistency and phased understanding to how change is managed and implemented. One such framework is ADKAR which stands for Awareness, Desire, Knowledge, Ability and Reinforcement. This framework illustrates the stages that an organization needs to go through in order to implement lasting, effective change.

Change Agents

Many times, Experience Brands are started as a corporate development or executive management initiative. This is when a small group of change agents are pulled together to lead the organization toward a new vision.

Cross Functional Stakeholder Engagement

The change agents leading the charge will need support and leadership from multiple stakeholders across the organization. By establishing a cross-functional stakeholder organization or committee, your Experience Brand strategy will gain the visibility and support needed to get started and execute accordingly. This Cross-Functional Stakeholder group is emboldened not only to make decisions on behalf of the organization, but also is accountable for communicating the process and the outcomes to the broader organization.

Meeting Structure – Standups

To ensure ongoing communication, transparency, and accountability, the Change Agents and Cross-Functional Stakeholder group need to meet openly on an extremely regular basis to communicate how work streams are evolving, what barriers they are running into, what they need from each other, and what they've been learning along the way. From my experience the working level team should have daily "standups," while the broader, Cross-Functional Stakeholder group should have weekly business plan reviews. The outcomes or minutes from these meetings should be made available for others in the organization to have insight into what is happening.

Project Tracking – RYG

To support the ongoing tracking and documentation of the Strategic Roadmap initiatives, it is important to implement a tracking mechanism for current status, what's happening, what the barriers are, and whether the work stream is on track. One tool that works great for this is a simple Red Yellow Green (RYG) Tracker. This living and breathing dashboard shows the details of the holistic progress while detailing each initiative in a way that shows whether it's on track or not. Red, meaning the work stream is off track. Yellow means it's at risk of going off track. Green means it's on track.

Innovation Accounting: Wins, Losses, Lessons

Finally, the best way to gain momentum for the Experience Brand strategy initiatives is to illustrate the progress the initiatives are making in terms of Wins, Losses, and Lessons. This innovation-accounting approach gives the organization valuable insight into the brand, the consumer, and the outcomes of tests, and provides the ability to make stronger business decisions, find new value opportunities, or learn more about the consumer.

CHANGE IS IN THE WIND

Making change requires a systematic approach to doing things differently on a daily basis. It's a combination of consistency and persistence that creates the momentum that expands with learning and success. By using a tried and true framework like ADKAR and methodologies like Lean Startup, Experience Brands can create a culture of evolution, moving beyond a linear, traditional, manufacturing mindset. Implementing this agility into the organizational culture, creates the ability to quickly and systematically transform, and sets up the organization for success through measurement, learning, and evolution.

www.JourneyEconomy.com/chapter-12

#changemanagement@PaulMiser

LESSONS LEARNED

- Change Management is a whole-of-organization approach to implementing the Experience Brand strategy. Leveraging the Lean Startup Methodology, operationalizing communication and implementing the right tools, organizations can embrace the transformation for the change at hand and also prepare for evolutionary change.
- Lean Startup Methodology is a tried and true approach to evolutionary transformation. From MVPs (minimum viable products), to consumer testing, to rapid decision making, this methodology holds power for all sizes of organizations.
- Operationalizing Communication about the vision is one thing; keeping ongoing communication lines open around the process as well as the outcomes is something completely different. It opens transparency, aids in accountability, and opens the ability for collaboration and innovation.
- Doing things differently requires different tools for success and implementation.

CHAPTER 13

MEASURE, OPTIMIZE, EVOLVE

MAXIMIZING YOUR WINNINGS IN THE JOURNEY ECONOMY

"Change is inevitable. Evolution, however, is optional."
Tony Robbins

AS CONSUMER expectations continue to rise and technology continues to advance, companies must find ways to innovate to stay ahead of their customers. This innovation will happen within the experience of the brand to find new ways to deliver value within current products and services as well as find new products and services to offer consumers. As consumers evolve, so must the experience. It's the company's responsibility to continuously make this happen.

There is a term that is being used now called "Continuous Beta," which I really like. It's the assumption that a business is continuously striving to create new value and new relationships in the marketplace based on an operational process of Launch, Test, Learn, Grow. The companies that are thriving today can all be viewed as companies that are in continuous beta, always striving for better.

Whether it's Amazon implementing and evolving Prime, or Google testing new products like Glass, or Microsoft continuously iterating and connecting their products based on consumer usage and feedback, each company is continuously evolving and working toward creating a new future.

To create a culture of Continuous Beta or evolution, Experience Brands deploy a system of Measure-Optimize-Evolve built on the back of the implementation approach we covered in Chapter 12. This approach systematically and strategically ushers your brand and your relationships to new heights by continuous learning, data-driven decision making, and consumer relationship management. Experience Brands are experts at playing and succeeding in the Infinite Game— always striving for, but never fully achieving, enlightenment.

MEASURE

The lifeblood that sustains the Experience Brand is the insights it gathers through continuously measuring, testing, and learning. However, knowing what to measure, how to measure, how to recognize an insight, and what to do with that insight is something that Experience Brands continuously strive to perfect. In this world of "big data" we have become encumbered with analytics and metrics, often not making sense or usable in any way. Building on the Experience Brand strategy and the Strategic Roadmap, Experience Brands have clarity in the value they are providing for their consumers, where their brand is going, and what outcomes they need in order to continuously add value along the entire consumer journey. This explicit intentionality gives Experience Brands the framework to best measure and garner the right information for optimization and evolution.

Curriculum of Measure and Learn

As the strategic roadmap is established and operationalized for the organization, there is a built-in curriculum for learning. This curriculum is based on solving the jobs to be done for the consumers throughout the journey, and it has explicit actions to be executed as the strategies are implemented. This curriculum includes hypotheses, metrics, and decision trees based on outcomes.

Consumer Feedback Loop

Experience Brands open the dialog with their consumers to continuously gather feedback in many different respects. First, Experience Brands test everything before, during, and after launch—from concept, to prototype, to live strategy. Experience Brands establish beta consumer sets to continuously test these ideas to gather feedback along the entire process of development and implementation. Second, there are built in feedback loops in the strategy, platforms, or products that are developed to interact with the consumer; if the consumer interacts with an app, the app has the ability to ask for and capture feedback. Finally, Experience Brands gather passive activity from their consumers based on their organic action. This activity can include website analytics, store foot traffic, and customer support data, among other actions. Each action has a data point that is measurable. Each strategic initiative is trying to solve for these interactions. Experience Brands continuously measure and learn through this consumer feedback loop.

Ongoing Trend Analysis

As stated before, a factor for success of Experience Brands is their ability to identify and capitalize on new opportunities in the Journey Economy. These opportunities can be found in many different forms—from consumer feedback, or technological advances, or consumer behavioral shifts. Experience Brands have a unique ability to keep their thumb on the pulse of culture to best understand where opportunities might unfold. As hockey great Wayne Gretzky says, "I skate to where the puck is going, not where it has been." Experience Brands employ this same mindset across the entire Journey Economy.

Competitive: Experience Brands look at the first, second, and tertiary degrees of competition to see what products, services, or experiences are launching that may disrupt or open opportunities for their organizations. They look at established players, reinvented incumbents, and even disruptive startups.

Technological Advancements: Technology is advancing faster and faster with each new innovation. From Artificial Intelligence, to Machine Learning, to 5G technology, the acceleration of technology will continuously open opportunities to add more importance to the consumer experience through efficiency, effectiveness, or value proposition.

Consumer Behaviors: As we've been witnessing in the Journey Economy, the expectations and behaviors consumers are creating in one industry affect all industries. The ease of hailing an Uber has a direct effect on fast-food restaurant expectations. These behavioral shifts not only change the expectations consumers have with brands; they create new value in how the consumer journey should unfold.

Business: Businesses change. As products, services and experiences from your business evolve, so will the expectation and value-proposition opportunities. Experience Brands use these changes to establish new business models to better serve their consumers while adding value to the bottom line.

OPTIMIZE

Using the data collected through ongoing measurement of strategic implementation and opportunities found through ongoing trend analysis, Experience Brands make business decisions to capitalize on mega trends and consumer behavior. These decisions may range from something as small as optimizing a process to become more efficient and effective, all the way to starting a new business unit to capture a new market value proposition. The way that Experience Brands leverage insights is the key to their ongoing success as an organization, creating exponential growth.

Consumer Journey

In the Journey Economy, the path the consumer goes through to do business with the brands they purchase is becoming as valuable as the product or service itself. By continuously refining and redefining their Consumer Journey Map, Experience

Brands can ensure they are continuously adding value to their customers while staying ahead of trends.

Optimize Activities

From marketing, to transaction, to supply chain, to logistics, to support, there is value in becoming incrementally efficient and effective. Using the data and insights captured, Experience Brands are always optimizing their processes, procedures, and messaging. These incremental optimizations, over time, create massive value for the organization and the consumer experience.

Keep, Kill, Pivot, Scale

One thing that is crucial to the future success of Experience Brands is the ability to move beyond legacy and old business models. Using data and trend analysis, Experience Brands are continuously making the decisions to keep, kill, pivot, or scale their strategies. If the opportunity for increased consumer value changes, Experience Brands are ready to take immediate action, with no emotional connection to what was, what is, or what might be. The main focus is to continuously add value to the consumer relationship.

Decision Making

When white-space opportunities show themselves in the data, across the consumer journey, or within mega trends, Experience Brands have the agility and ability to make swift decisions and create new businesses, products, or services. These decisions are rooted in insights and data and are enabled by their Experience Brand strategy. Whether it's Nike moving to a subscription model, or Amazon buying a department store, these decisions are extensions of their Experience Brand strategy. By expanding Vertically or Horizontally, or by Bundling or Unbundling their offerings, decisions can be made quickly because of the principles, framework, and value propositions defined in the Experience Brand strategy.

EVOLVE

From an outsider's perspective, it seems that Experience Brands are continuously reinventing themselves at the right time for massive gains. However, this is just evolution at work. Evolution doesn't happen overnight. Rather it is a series of small events that make big changes over time. As we've seen, Experience Brands are dedicated to learning, growing, and evolving along with opportunity and their consumers by establishing their North Star strategy, their principles and framework. Experience Brands have a continuously developing value proposition that is never truly fulfilled. However, with the consistency and persistence to fulfill their brand promise, these Experience Brands are rising to new heights as they evolve, creating more and more value in the Journey Economy, and expanding their moat in the marketplace.

Self-Actualization

The final horizon of brand strategy is one of Self-Actualization. This is the ability to truly know who we are, why we're here, and to act in accordance with that role and structure in the world. This self-actualization of an Experience Brand is not only a singular expression from the brand entity, but a collection of individuals, processes, and technologies that expands the value, understanding, and actions needed to bring it to life. It's a symbiotic ecosystem that lives, breathes, interacts, and evolves with its environment, the Journey Economy.

Relationship Management

The power of self-actualization for the exchange between brand and consumer is a personalized relationship. This relationship is established through ongoing opt-in opportunities and trust built from using preference and data correctly to exceed expectations over the course of time. The more singular the experience, the more personalized the interaction, the stronger the relationship between consumer and brand. Experience Brands don't think of their brand as an advertiser or a marketer, but as a dynamic relationship manager, ensuring their value proposition comes to life holistically as well as on an individual level. Leveraging data and technology, Experience Brands can create these relationships at scale.

Recurring Revenue

Value is being created in many different ways by brands. However, the companies that create the most symbiotic value with their consumers witness exponential increases in long-term, lifetime value. Many Experience Brands deploy business models that deliver recurring revenue, instantly increasing both economic value and relationship responsibility for the consumer. This business model of the future hits on many points throughout this book, but none more than truly living with a membership mindset. By building relationships with consumers as members, Experience Brands continuously create new value in the Journey Economy.

The Infinite Game

As we wrap up our journey together, there is one final aspect of the Experience Brand evolution. That is the culture and strategy of continuously adding value to the consumer and the relationship. Whether it's making it easier to do business with you, personally celebrating moments of joy, or creating new products for a market, Experience Brands never lose sight of the true goal—adding value. By viewing your brand as an infinite game, you'll not only keep moving, but you'll keep learning, growing, and evolving.

INCREMENTALLY INNOVATING

The true power of becoming an Experience Brand is the ability to continuously evolve your consumer relationships for increased value exchanges between your consumer and your brand. This ability to continuously evolve is an intentional system and framework of measure, optimize, and evolve. By using ongoing quantitative and qualitative research methodologies and trends analysis, Experience Brands gain firsthand insight in the needs and opportunities provided by consumer behavior shifts and macro opportunities.

By capitalizing on these varying degrees of insight and opportunity, Experience Brands will incrementally expand over time, while leveraging white-space trends to create step-change innovation.

www.JourneyEconomy.com/chapter-13

#evolution@PaulMiser

LESSONS LEARNED

- Experience Brands live with the worldview of Continuous Beta, always evolving their value proposition to better serve their consumers through the entirety of the consumer journey. This Continuous Beta mindset is rooted in the framework of ongoing measure, optimize, and evolve.

- Experience Brands know what to measure to move the needle on their daily activity and also to know which levers to pull for step-change growth. By creating an ongoing, holistic view of data, from qualitative, to quantitative, to trends analysis, Experience Brands have their finger on the pulse of their consumers and opportunity.

- Optimization is using data to incrementally change strategies and activities to become more efficient or more effective. This could be A/B testing ads, making a checkout with less friction, changing the size and color of a button to perform better, or reducing the touch points needed to service a product. Each of these decisions are rooted in data, while incrementally transforming the brand toward the Experience Brand vision.

- Evolution happens when the qualitative, quantitative, and trends analysis uncover white-space opportunities for growth. These could come about through consumer behavior shifts, competitive action, technological transformation, or other macro movements. However, the response from an Experience Brand gives the opportunity context, texture, and power to completely evolve the strategy and value proposition it's providing.

EPILOGUE

"Perfection of character is this: to live each day as if it were your last, without frenzy, without apathy, without pretense."
Marcus Aurelius

IF THERE is anything we've learned in the last five years, and if the COVID-19 pandemic in 2020 were any teacher, change is inevitable—and it can happen gradually or instantaneously. The triggers for change are always ebbing and flowing in and out of our business environment and consumer's lives. There is no guarantee that what worked yesterday will work today. There has become fluidity in industries with new market insurgents, adjacent value propositions, and shifting consumer needs. Technological advances are happening at a pace never seen before. Moore's Law is truly in full effect and there's no sign of slowing.

These elements are creating a sense of acceleration of time—something that our brands and organizations aren't traditionally set up to capitalize on. Leading with a manufacturing mindset, traditional organizations have long been methodical, linear, and optimizing. Experience Brands are built with agility at their core. They use systems and frameworks to solve for consumer pain points that may not be directly related with their core products or services, and they look to their consumer interactions to gain insight for new value propositions to add to the consumer relationship.

The progression of consumer expectations, expanding with first, second, and third-level industry interactions, are creating a new level of responsibility and accountability for brands. Consumers are expecting value beyond products and services and aligning with the brands that give them more throughout their consumer journey in terms of experience. By saving them time, making them feel like a valued member, or simply maintaining a relationship with them on an individual level, consumer expectations are moving from mass to personal across all aspects of business. This forces brands to create a singular experience across the entirety of the organization.

The true growth opportunity for brands moving forward is to fully realize their potential within the Journey Economy by expanding focus of value, away from products and services, toward experiences, and by expanding their interactions from advertising toward personalized moments of value creation. Experience Brands have proven to find exponential growth in uncertain times, times of expansion, and as we're witnessing now, moments of complete shutdown. This growth isn't luck. It's by design. It's an intentional decision to prepare a brand for agility and continuously add value to their consumers.

Every brand, including yours, has this same opportunity. I hope the previous pages have given you the insight, the knowledge, the strategies, and the inspiration to capitalize on this opportunity. I wish you continued success and look forward to watching your transformation to becoming an Experience Brand.

 **RESOURCE GUIDE**

MANY of the elements and touchpoints you develop for your Experience Brand strategy will be bespoke to your brand. However, there are many tools, products and platforms that can be used off the shelf to implement for your Experience Brand. This Resource Guide is a starting point to get you on your way. You can view an updated and ever-evolving Resource Guide on www.JourneyEconomy.com as well as tools to help you and your organization through the Experience Brand strategy transformation.

STRATEGIC ROADMAPPING

Developing the overarching project list and project plan to execute the various stages of your Experience Brand strategy.

Planview LeanKit: https://www.planview.com/products-solutions/products/leankit/

LeanKit enables engineering teams across all levels of the organization with a visual work delivery tool to apply Lean management principles to their work, helping them work smarter and deliver faster.

ProductPlan: https://www.productplan.com/

ProductPlan is a collaborative platform that allows cross-functional teams to build a product roadmap and the necessary documentation and deliverables to fulfill the roadmap.

roadmunk: https://roadmunk.com/

Roadmunk is an end-to-end roadmapping tool. It allows users to capture customer feedback and prioritize what to build next. And use boardroom-ready roadmaps to communicate your strategy.

CUSTOMER / MARKET RESEARCH

Experience Brands are obsessed with learning about and understanding their customers. Using the right tools will help uncover new insights and opportunities for your customers.

Google Trends: https://trends.google.com/

Google Trends is a website by Google that analyzes the popularity of top search queries in Google Search across various regions and languages. The website uses graphs to compare the search volume of different queries over time.

Qualtrics: https://www.qualtrics.com/market-research/

Qualtrics Market Research is a platform that leverage AI to uncover insights. With many different feature sets like market segmentation, product development, purchase behavior and a/b testing, Qualtrics Market Research is a robust solution for market research.

Upwave: https://www.upwave.com/

Upwave is a predictive analytics platform that measures cross-channel brand campaigns.

Global Web Index (GWI): https://www.globalwebindex.com/

GWI is a data and intelligence platform that delivers off-the-shelf market insights from ongoing index panels with the ability to segment based on audience details.

AUDIENCE & PERSONA DEVELOPMENT

Using ongoing customer and market research, Experience Brands build deep and actionable audience segments and personas. By understanding the nuance of customer segments and building a definitive persona gives Experience Brands a starting point to customer experience and personalization.

Xtensio: https://xtensio.com/

Xtensio is a business document collaboration platform that has templates for persona development.

Make My Persona by Hubspot: https://www.hubspot.com/make-my-persona

Make My Persona is an online tool that creates actionable personas based on a series of questions and inputs.

User Forge: https://userforge.com/

User Forge is an online platform that helps create real life personas and user stories.

CUSTOMER JOURNEY MAPPING, SERVICE DESIGN & PROCESS MAPS

Experience Brands make their personas actionable by mapping current and ideal customer journeys. These maps illustrate the journeys their high value audiences take to do business with their brands. They become the foundation for their Experience Brand strategy — uncovering opportunities to reduce pain points and maximize moments of cherish. With this understanding, new services and processes will be developed to bring the customer experience to life.

Flowmapp: https://www.flowmapp.com/

Flowmapp is a series of user experience tools that make customer experience actionable — from sitemap development to user flows to personas to customer journey maps.

Medallia: https://www.medallia.com/

Medallia is a suite of tools for the customer experience journey. From journey mapping, to service design, to employee empowerment to customer experience journey analytics, Medallia is an end-to-end tool.

Smaply: https://www.smaply.com/

Smaply is an online tool for customer journey, persona and stakeholder mapping allowing you to visualize your customers' experience.

IBM Automation: https://www.ibm.com/cloud/automation

IBM Automation uses AI to map, deliver and optimize business workflows and IT processes — creating a more efficient and effective customer experience.

DESIGN / PROTOTYPING

Once areas of opportunity are identified, a digital product may be needed to expand or activate Experience Brands. Following lean startup methodology, the cycle of design, prototype and test is leveraged to ensure whatever is being built truly creates the expected value for the customer or the organization.

Adobe Creative Cloud: https://www.adobe.com/creativecloud.html
Adobe Creative Cloud is a suite of tools that give brands the ability to design and develop all types of products, including prototypes.

axure: https://www.axure.com/
axure is a prototyping tool that turns designs into prototypes to hand off to developers.

Sketch: https://www.sketch.com/
Sketch is a design toolkit that has the ability to create immersive prototypes and hand off to development.

invision: https://www.invisionapp.com/
invision is a digital product design platform that is focused on user experience and immersive prototypes.

Figma: https://www.figma.com/
Figma is a collaborative design tool that allows for designing, prototyping and user testing.

USER TESTING / FEEDBACK

Testing solutions in market and gathering ongoing feedback from customers gives Experience Brands the ability to continuously refine their offering, engaging their customers and uncovering new insights along the way.

usertesting: https://www.usertesting.com/
usertesting is a platform to gather user insights for new products, marketing and general market. Its platform provides the ability for brands to test concepts and prototypes.

Hotjar: https://www.hotjar.com/
Hotjar is a tool to gather passive and active behavioral analytics from users across different digital products.

Qualtrics: https://www.qualtrics.com/core-xm/website-app-feedback-surveys/
Qualtrics is a suite of customer experience management tools — from analytics and surveys to product market fit to concept testing to analytics.

Parlor: https://www.parlor.io/
Parlor is an analytics platform that records and captures insights across the entire customer journey.

BUSINESS MODEL TESTING

Before investing in a massive overhaul of an organization or business unit, Experience Brands leverage tools to continuously test business models before implementing change.

Strategyzer: https://www.strategyzer.com/
Strategyzer is a company that has tools, consulting and resources to help companies create, test and optimize business models and value propositions.

MARKETING AUTOMATION

When implemented, many elements of the Experience Brand activity can and should be automated to achieve consistency and scale. Combining technology and human resources effectively.

Pardot: https://www.pardot.com/
Pardot, a part of Salesforce, is a B2B marketing automation software that allows brands to create customized cross-channel experiences, then automate them.

Adobe Experience Cloud: https://www.adobe.com/experience-cloud.html
Adobe Experience Cloud is a suite of tools for end-to-end customer experience design and management driving towards personalization.

Eloqua: https://www.oracle.com/cx/marketing/automation/
Eloqua, a part of Oracle, is a marketing automation software that allows brands to generate robust customer experiences based on audience segments and detailed triggers.

Hubspot: https://www.hubspot.com/products/marketing/marketing-automation
Hubspot Marketing Automation software creates automated workflows for marketing across many different channels.

Salsify: https://www.salsify.com/
Salsify is an end-to-end commerce experience platform that manages many different digital retail experiences.

BUSINESS INTELLIGENCE

Experience Brands are innately data-driven, whether with customer data or through analytics and insights. Business Intelligence is crucial to the implementation and expansion of any Experience Brand strategy.

Qlik: https://www.qlik.com/
Qlik is a business intelligence platform that enables data integration and delivers data visualization for many aspects of a business.

Tableau: https://www.tableau.com/
Tableau is a data visualization and analytics platform used to uncover insights from big data.

Power BI: https://powerbi.microsoft.com/
Power BI is Microsoft's data visualization tool — creating rich visuals and reports for better insights and understanding of a business.

Datorama: https://datorama.com/
Datorama, a Salesforce company, is an AI-powered marketing and business intelligence platform providing data integration and a marketplace for standardized reporting and analytics.

IBM Cognos Analytics: https://www.ibm.com/analytics/business-intelligence

IBM Cognos Analytics is an AI-powered business intelligence and analytics software that supports the entire data analytics lifecycle.

Domo: https://www.domo.com/

Domo Business Cloud is a business intelligence platform that takes many different data sources, including live data to create reports and visualizations.

CUSTOMER ONBOARDING

Getting customers to purchase a product or service is one thing; getting them onboarded into a brand or experience is something that has lasting impact for Experience Brands.

Pendo: https://www.pendo.io/

Pendo is a product onboarding platform that drives product adoption, customer loyalty and team innovation.

Whatfix: https://whatfix.com/

Whatfix is a product onboarding experience that delivers adoption of enterprise applications for employees.

WalkMe: https://www.walkme.com/

WalkMe is a Digital Adoption Platform to simplify online experiences and drive adoption.

COMMERCE & TRANSACTIONS

As commerce is happening Anytime and Anywhere, having the right commerce tools provides flexibility and scalability for Experience Brands, bringing commerce to the customer. There are many different types of point-of-sale solutions from Google Pay and ApplePay to platform integrations like Sitecore Commerce or Shopify. Some include:

Square: https://squareup.com/

Square is a commerce and transaction platform that allows businesses to sell in person or online.

Shopify: https://www.shopify.com/

Shopify is an ecommerce platform that allows anyone to start and grow an ecommerce business.

Lightspeed: https://www.lightspeedhq.com/

Lightspeed is a point-of-sale platform for retail and restaurants.

IMMERSIVE COMMERCE

Commerce is blending the physical with the digital. Immersive platforms give Experience Brands the ability to provide new shopping experiences for customers.

Bitreel: https://www.bitreel.com/

Bitreel is an immersive 3D virtual shopping experience platform that allows brands and retailers to create virtual showrooms and experiences for their customers.

Arthur: https://arthur.digital/

Arthur is a virtual office space that allows organizations and teams to meet, collaborate and manage work.

ByondXR: https://www.byondxr.com/

ByondXR is a virtual showroom for different industries and products. The platform includes a 3D home visualizer for real-life immersive experiences.

CONSUMER EXPERIENCE MANAGEMENT

The true success factor for Experience Brands is the ability to orchestrate the entire customer experience across the organization.

Adobe Experience Cloud: https://www.adobe.com/experience-cloud.html

Adobe Experience Cloud is a suite of tools for end-to-end customer experience design and management driving towards personalization.

Qualtrics: https://www.qualtrics.com/

Qualtrics is a suite of customer experience management tools — from analytics and surveys to product market fit to concept testing to analytics.

Medallia: https://www.medallia.com/

Medallia is a suite of tools for the customer experience journey. From journey mapping, to service design, to employee empowerment to customer experience journey analytics, Medallia is an end-to-end tool.

Sitecore: https://www.sitecore.com/

Sitecore is a Digital Experience Platform used to connect data science and marketing technology to bring customer experiences to life.

Thunderhead: https://www.thunderhead.com/

Thunderhead is a customer journey orchestration tool that delivers real-time interaction management solutions.

Wootric Customer Experience: https://www.wootric.com/

Wootric is an experience management software to deliver relevant customer experiences across a set of customer experience measures like Net Promotor Score and Customer Satisfaction Score.

CUSTOMER DATA PLATFORMS

Customer data is the lifeblood of Experience Brands. Utilizing a customer data platform gives Experience Brands the ability to store and activate various types of customer data across first party, second party and third party.

Exponea: https://exponea.com/

Exponea is a customer data platform that delivers email management and predictive analytics for personalized customer experience.

Segment: https://segment.com/

Segment, a Twilio company, collects user data with one API to send it to hundreds of tools or data sources.

Amperity: https://amperity.com/

Amperity is a customer data platform that measures and collects data across the entire customer journey process for customer intelligence, activation and ROI measurement.

LOYALTY & MEMBERSHIP

Experience Brands work with the mindset of extreme loyalty and membership, moving their customers beyond a single transaction and into an ongoing relationship.

Annex Cloud: https://www.annexcloud.com/

Annex Cloud is a loyalty experience management platform that drives customer retention and rewards.

Talon One: https://www.talon.one/

Talone.One is an all-in-one promotion platform to deliver scalable and flexible solutions for brands.

Qualtrics: https://www.qualtrics.com/

Qualtrics is a suite of customer experience management tools — from analytics and surveys to product market fit to concept testing to analytics.

Medallia: https://www.medallia.com/

Medallia is a suite of tools for the customer experience journey. From journey mapping, to service design, to employee empowerment to customer experience journey analytics, Medallia is an end-to-end tool.

INDEX

ABOUT THE AUTHOR

 **PAUL MISER** is a seasoned digital business professional with almost two decades as an entrepreneur and intrapreneur—building global brands and organizations at the forefront of technology. Leveraging digital technologies, methodologies and processes, Miser's strategic framework helps companies develop a long-term vision with short-term action and immediate growth.

Currently, Miser is the CEO of Chinatown Bureau, a growth strategy agency, and Chief Strategy Officer of its parent company Icreon, a digital solutions agency. Together, Chinatown Bureau and Icreon have developed an Acceleration Studio that guides brands to see their consumer relationships in a new, profitable way—solving their biggest growth challenges through Go to Market, Consumer Experience, Commerce and Business Model strategies.

Prior to starting Chinatown Bureau, Miser spent his career in advertising firms like VMLY&R and Hudson Rouge where he built multi-million-dollar business units innovating, establishing, and operationalizing technology for real business and brand growth. These businesses included an outsourced digital marketing agency, an innovation and emerging media lab, a brand content publishing organization, and a consumer experience and product development accelerator.

Working with clients like Lincoln, Ford, Novartis, Tempur Sealy, Colgate-Palmolive, LG and Xerox, Miser has not only delivered industry-leading business growth in complex organizations, but also has been recognized globally by Cannes Lions, the Clios, the Webby's, the One Club, and the Effie Awards.

Miser lives in New York City with his wife and daughter. He is a graduate of Northwest Missouri State University in Maryville, Missouri, where he received his Bachelor's of Science in Business Management and Marketing as well as his MBA.